A Boring Evening
at Home

A Boring Evening at Home

Gerda Weissmann Klein

Washington, DC

ALSO by Gerda Weissmann Klein

All But My Life: A Memoir

The Hours After: Letters of Love and Longing in War's Aftermath

The Blue Rose

Promise of a New Spring

A Passion for Sharing

Leading Authorities Press
1220 L Street, N.W.
Suite 850
Washington, DC 20005-4070
202-783-0300
www.leadingauthorities.com

ISBN 0-9710078-8-8

I have often been told that my life resembles
Cinderella's. I do not deny it. But, in the fairy tale, the
spotlight is always on Cinderella, and scant attention
is given to the prince who transformed her life into—
"and they lived happily ever after." Therefore, I
dedicate my life's story to my beloved prince.

G.W.K.

Contents

Foreword

*T*HE ESSAYS IN THIS BOOK ESSENTIALLY STAND ON THEIR OWN without much need of explanation. But because they are written in such a personal style, a brief review of the lives of the author and her husband, as well as their perspectives on life, may allow the reader to appreciate the stories more fully and to consider them in their proper context. As the author's son, I make no pretense of being unbiased. But what my views may lack in objectivity is, I hope, more than compensated by both my knowledge of the author, and my having been familiar with these stories for a very long time. In preparing this foreword, I consulted with my two sisters, Vivian Ullman and Leslie Simon. And so these reflections represent their thoughts as well as my own.

OUR FATHER, KURT KLEIN, WAS BORN IN 1920 in Walldorf, Germany. His rather normal boyhood was arrested when the Nazis came to power in 1933. As conditions worsened for Jews, it became apparent that he would have to leave in order to survive. His parents and his sister, Gerdi, were finally able to arrange his safe passage to the United States, specifically, to Buffalo, New York, to which his uncle and aunt had previously immigrated. Though his sister and brother, Max, did survive, along with a number of cousins, aunts, and uncles, many of their relatives perished. Dad and his siblings were ultimately unsuccessful in saving their parents from their tragic fate. Dad's story, and that of his parents, is recounted in the PBS documentary *America and*

the Holocaust: Deceit and Indifference.

Our mother, Gerda Weissmann Klein, was born in Bielsko, Poland, in 1924, and her very protected childhood came to an even more sudden halt than our father's in September 1939 when the Nazis invaded her hometown. For the next six years, she endured the horrors of the Holocaust in a series of slave labor camps and a death march of several hundred miles during the final months of World War II. Her parents, her adored older brother, Artur, and virtually her entire family perished. Hence the title of her autobiography recounting both the events and losses of those years: *All But My Life.*

WHILE MOM AND DAD'S EXPERIENCES AND THEIR FAMILY'S FATE were, unfortunately, all too common, the circumstances of their meeting were unusual. By war's end, Dad was an intelligence officer in the U.S. Army Fifth Infantry Division, and he commanded the unit that liberated Mom and the remnant of survivors of the death march in Volary, Czechoslovakia, in May 1945. While it was not quite a case of "love at first sight," they evidently both immediately made an impression on each other. As Dad frequently noted in the years that followed, there was some quality of Mom's demeanor under such unspeakable conditions that struck a responsive chord within him. For Mom, too, that very night of her liberation she said a prayer for the safety and well-being of this American soldier whose name she did not yet know. Over the ensuing four months, Dad looked after Mom as she recuperated in a hospital, and they fell in love. A year after their improbable meeting, Mom not only knew Dad's last name but also took it as her own: They were married in Paris in June 1946. The story of their meeting, courtship, engagement, nine-month-long separation, and efforts to be reunited and married—as told through their extraordinary letters to each other—is the focus of the book they coauthored: *The Hours After: Letters of Love and Longing in War's Aftermath.*

In a sense, the rest, as they say, is history. Dad brought Mom back to Buffalo, where they made their home for the next thirty-nine years.

During this time, Dad owned a printing business and Mom represented the epitome of a "career woman," mastering the art of "multitasking" long before either term became part of our everyday lexicon. Incredibly, Mom delivered her first public speech just weeks after arriving in the United States—and she has never stopped. She not only wrote her autobiography but also a number of other books on varied topics, and for many years, she wrote a weekly column for young readers in the *Buffalo News*. She managed to accomplish all these professional successes, and more, while at the same time juggling an immense array of domestic pursuits from PTA to carpools to always throwing *the* most creative parties (the first of which is recounted in the story "New Year's Eve"). In 1985 Dad retired, and our parents moved to Scottsdale, Arizona. In many respects the seventeen years that followed were the most enriched ones for Mom and Dad; most especially because they were able to spend virtually all that time with each other. Much more frequently than before, they were able to collaborate on writing projects and speaking engagements.

STARTING SOMETIME IN THE 1960S, and over the course of the following decades, Mom had written some vignettes of her postwar life since arriving in the United States. Over the years she published one or two of them in the *Buffalo News*, but mostly they reposed in a file folder waiting to be published in collected book form "someday"—when the hectic pace of our parents' lives would allow them to get around to it.

In the mid-1990s, following the release of the PBS documentary, produced by Marty Ostrow, about Dad's experiences, and the release of Kary Antholis's Academy Award-winning HBO documentary, *One Survivor Remembers*, recounting Mom's experiences, our parents' "retirement" moved into even higher gear. Their lecture itinerary took them, literally, around the world. Despite the frenetic pace, however, they managed to find time to entertain an endless stream of guests in Scottsdale and to devote more time than ever to family.

ALTHOUGH WE ALWAYS HAD GREAT FAMILY VACATIONS while we were growing up, Mom and Dad truly outdid themselves in the summer of 2000 with a phenomenal trip with all the children and grandchildren to celebrate Dad's eightieth birthday. Mom was the motivating force for this reckless extravagance, against Dad's typical reluctance that a big fuss be made over him. He finally relented, insisting on one condition: He did not want to take the family any place in the world where Mom had ever cried— either tears of grief or joy. Given Mom's oft-stated propensity to cry even at supermarket ribbon-cutting ceremonies, that pretty much limited the choice of destinations to places Mom and Dad had never been. And thus, all sixteen of us celebrated Dad's special birthday with a cruise through French Polynesia.

It was during one of the dinners aboard ship that we asked Dad what wisdom he might impart to us, gleaned from eighty years of experience. After just a short pause, he said that while it is important to strive for accomplishments, real happiness comes from the ability and wisdom to be content with your station in life if you have done your best. Readers of this book will find complementary messages in many of Mom's stories.

In the midst of their busy lives, by the winter of 2002, Mom and Dad had actually begun to move forward on *finally* assembling and, where necessary, updating the stories Mom had written over the years. Some of them had not been touched since they were first pounded out on the old Smith-Corona typewriter in our home in Buffalo. They took along several of these stories as they flew to Central America for a lecture tour and vacation in El Salvador and Guatemala in April 2002. On the plane, Dad plied his own literary talents as he edited the stories, and Mom showed him the dedication—to him—she had written, which appears in this book. A few days later, while they vacationed in Guatemala, Dad suffered a heart attack, and only Mom's quick response kept him alive until the ambulance could get him to the hospital. Over the next few days, the tiny but wonderful Jewish community of Guatemala City— and especially newfound friends, Dina and Mario Nathusius—enveloped Mom and Dad in its warmth, and Dad seemed to recover quickly.

Vivian, Leslie, her husband Roger, daughter Julie, and I flew to Guatemala to see Dad and to keep Mom company. Dad looked great, took phone calls from concerned family members, inquired about the grandchildren's activities, and, quite typically, put the rest of us to shame with his innate linguistic abilities, carrying on a repartee in Spanish with his nurses—even though he did not speak Spanish! As plans were being made for his release from the hospital, he was fatally stricken with another heart attack.

NEEDLESS TO SAY, FOR THE NEXT SEVERAL MONTHS Mom's public speaking and writing, including the work on this book, abruptly stopped as she coped with the incomprehensible loss of her life's partner. But in tribute to Dad, who believed in both the vital importance of their life's work as well as Mom's unique ability to convey eloquently their message of tolerance, hope, and the redemptive power of love, Mom has somehow mustered the strength to go on. She has returned to the lecture circuit, albeit with less joy than when Dad was at her side sharing the podium. Despite the difficulty, she has been true to the creed to which she and Dad subscribed, that "pain should not be wasted." Over the past several months, Mom has worked with her editor and publisher and her family to finish this book, as Dad would have wanted. She and we hope that it is a product of which he would be proud—from the editing of the stories to the selection of the typeface. He not only made his career as the owner of a printing business, but he was also trained in Germany as a typesetter; so we know that he would have thoroughly enjoyed *every* aspect of the development of this book.

BUT WHAT OF THE BOOK ITSELF? What is its fundamental purpose and message?

It is not an easy task to take the measure of a person's life. It should certainly be judged in its totality and not by either its greatest or lowest moments, but what Mom and Dad themselves noted were their greatest accomplishments provides a glimpse into their characters and the themes that hopefully come through in this collection of essays. Not surprisingly, our parents were frequently asked what they considered their greatest accomplishments. Like most parents, they would typically answer with the honest yet obligatory, "raising our children." But on a couple of occasions, they opened a window into their deeper selves with more revealing answers.

Despite the accolades, awards, and honorary doctorates of humane letters from no fewer than seven colleges and universities, Mom has noted to her family that she is proudest of the things she did during the war to assuage the pain of, and to give hope to, her parents and friends. The examples are too numerous to mention here, but one is illustrative. In the first slave camp in which she was interned, Bolkenhain, Mom would, after an exhausting day at the textile looms, sneak into the washroom at night. There, by the dim light of a single naked bulb hanging from the ceiling, she would write short plays on little scraps of paper. Later, during their few free moments in the barracks, she would organize and act in these plays to entertain her campmates. For some brief moments, it was her literary creativity and boundless imagination that would break the despair and loneliness of the hellish reality of their existence. For too, too many of those friends and acquaintances, Gerda Weissmann's words provided the last time in their lives that they smiled or laughed.

And what was Dad's greatest accomplishment? Certainly his wartime exploits were significant and unusual. As an intelligence officer charged with interrogating German prisoners of war, he had numerous fascinating experiences, including removing his own weapon and walking into an underground labyrinth filled with armed SS troops to tell them they needed to surrender, earning a Bronze Star; debriefing Ernest Hemingway, who arrived at Dad's office one morning with some captured German soldiers in tow; interrogating Adolf Hitler's chauffeur shortly after Hitler's suicide; and arranging for Oskar Schindler's safe passage to the American zone at war's end. That Dad did any or all of these things will probably come as a complete surprise to all of his friends and most of his family members, because the only "war story" he ever really cared to discuss was his luckiest moment: meeting Mom.

So what *did* Dad consider to be his greatest accomplishment? Ever a man of letters, he was justifiably proud of the honorary doctorate that he was awarded by Chapman University. He was not only a superb editor, but, as readers of the book he wrote with Mom will recognize, an accomplished writer himself. His poem, "Song of the Earth" (which is included here among Mom's stories) further attests to his literary prowess. But he himself answered the question about his greatest achievement in 1997 during remarks he delivered at ceremonies at Arizona State University, marking the fortieth anniversary of the publication of *All But My Life*. Dad recounted with love and humor his partnership with Mom in editing the drafts of the book and commented that over the many months of that work, he was keenly aware that his efforts in helping to ensure the publication of Mom's autobiography would be the most important thing he ever did.

My sisters and I have our own, admittedly nonobjective, view of our parents' greatest achievement. It is that they somehow managed, after surviving the crucible of the Holocaust, to create for themselves and their children a *normal* life. Defying both logic and vivid memories, they overcame incredible loss at a young age and surmounted their own pain and, yes, even their ill-deserved guilt (in Mom's case guilt that she survived, and in Dad's case guilt that he did not somehow manage to save his parents). Against all the odds, they maintained a sense of humor while never losing their sense of perspective. And they successfully shielded us from their anguish and created a home in which we all genuinely had a lot of fun and spent a lot of time laughing.

Remarkably, our parents became just regular American suburbanites, with many of the same hopes and dreams as their neighbors, and a variety of interests and friendships that in no way related to the Holocaust. Among those interests, Mom's splendid aptitude for history, especially British history, and Dad's exceptional knowledge of classical music and opera have left a particular impression on us, their children, whose academic opportunities far exceeded the eighth-grade educations that represented the culmination of our parents' formal schooling. Fortunately for both them and us, they accomplished everything they did, not by ignoring their past but, rather, by being among the first of Holocaust survivors to tell their stories publicly. They were both wise and lucky, that for them revealing even some of what lay beneath was cathartic and liberating.

THIS BOOK NEED NOT BE READ IN THE ORDER in which the stories are presented. Indeed, they are not set forth in the order in which they occurred or were written. Some of them have significant messages and powerful lessons. Others are simply interesting or amusing, perhaps because Mom has such a perceptive ability to see extraordinary meaning or juxtaposition in ordinary events. The stories provide insights on how to live with accomplishments as well as with regrets and disappointments; how to find joy and meaning in life's small moments as well as the large ones; how to overcome tragedy and loss and channel it into energy and commitment for positive change.

Ultimately, what Mom has done in this book is to share with a wider audience what her children and grandchildren have been privileged to learn directly from her, through her wisdom and insights as a mother, grandmother, adviser, and confidante. And that is that to cope with failure as much as to benefit from success, one must appreciate the magic of a boring evening at home.

James Arthur Weissmann Klein
Washington, D.C.
November 2003

Preface

I have been in a place for six incredible years, where winning meant a crust of bread and to live another day. Since the blessed day of my liberation I have asked the question, Why am I here? . . .

In my mind's eye, I see those years and the faces of those who never knew the magic of a boring evening at home. On their behalf, I wish to thank you for honoring their memory, and you cannot do that in a better way than when you return to your homes tonight to realize that each of you who knows the joy of freedom is a winner. On their behalf, I wish to thank you with all my heart.

—Remarks by Gerda Weissmann Klein,
acknowledging the Oscar for the documentary *One Survivor Remembers*, at the Sixty-eighth Annual Academy Awards in 1996

WHAT WERE MY THOUGHTS as I stood facing an audience comprising some of the most glamorous, privileged people on earth? In the glare of spotlights and amid the blaze of jewels, I held an Oscar in my hand, but my thoughts harked back to the icy, merciless winter days when I was on a death march during the last bitter months of World War II, holding a battered, rusty bowl in my hands. I was praying that when I finally got to the front of the line, there would be some food left in the kettle. And if the ladle went a little deeper and by some miracle brought forth a *potato*, I would be a winner!

I could not help but think that I do not want my grandchildren—or any children—to live in a world in which a potato is more valuable than an Oscar. Nor do I want them to live in a world in which an Oscar is so important that nobody cares whether some people still do not have a potato.

The key to my survival in the dark years of slavery was the memory of what had been before: memories of my family and my childhood. There was always one picture, which I would pull up from the deepest recesses of my mind and heart. I would hold it and examine it as one would a precious jewel. It was the memory of an evening at home. The picture was that of my childhood living room. Lamplight would softly illuminate the room, and in its warm glow, my father would be smoking his pipe, reading the evening paper, while my mother worked on her needlepoint. I could see my brother sprawled on the green carpet, doing his homework while I played with my cats. An evening at home—something I had taken utterly for granted. Seeing it from the perspective of my hard bunk, looking out at the barbed wire of the concentration camps, it became the most beautiful sight in the world. I was struck by the enormity of the fact that I had taken those evenings totally for granted, even thought of them as no more than "boring evenings at home."

That image became my lodestar, and I knew that I could endure anything to be part of one more evening at home with my family. It is a vision that has served me well throughout my life's journey. Coming home from even the more enviable places has never disappointed me, and being at home has always restored me whenever my spirits were flagging.

The following stories, then, are glimpses into my life, and into the thoughts that have always vindicated my belief that the most treasured place on earth is home, and that the most beautiful and desirable aim for me is to spend "a boring evening" there with my family.

Acknowledgments

MY GRATITUDE FOR THE EXISTENCE OF THIS BOOK goes first and foremost to Mark French, president of Leading Authorities, Inc. Mark not only suggested the title, which started my work to assemble in one place the many stories I had written over the years, but his enthusiasm and vision brought it to fruition. I am indebted to Matt Jones, also of Leading Authorities, whose wisdom, gentle prodding, and infinite patience were all essential to the completion of this project that means so much to me. Countless bouquets of appreciation are due to Susan Llewellyn, an extraordinary editor with unique insights and skills, who so effectively challenged me to consider each message and recollection—a particularly important element of this project, since some of the essays here had received little, if any, attention since I first wrote them decades ago. My special thanks to Sondra Williams, whom I hired to help with the typing; but who also rewarded me with her friendship. Al Gilens's artistic mastery is displayed in this book in the way he juxtaposed portions of a family photograph with the poem "Song of the Earth," written by my beloved husband, Kurt, and inspired by that photograph. I have had the good fortune of working with dear friends Ron Goldfarb, Beth Reisboard, and Nancy Fox on literary and other endeavors—Beth and Nancy also provide the vision and energy that makes possible the Gerda and Kurt Klein Foundation, which is dedicated to combating hunger and promoting tolerance. All three of them have regularly provided wise, thoughtful, and heartfelt advice that I always treasure.

I RECENTLY RETURNED TO BUFFALO, NEW YORK, for a visit and started to make a list of all those I wanted to acknowledge who have given me their friendship since I arrived, a stranger, in the city that I have called my true home since 1946. I want to express my gratitude for the care and thoughtfulness that has enriched my life over those many years. I would have liked to name individually not only my Buffalo friends, but also those from across the country and around the world who have really made a difference in my life. Their lives and friendship are the threads of which the fabric of my own life has been woven. I started jotting down names, and when I reached 183—far from the end of the list—I realized both the impossibility of this task and the guilt that I would feel if I listed names and then unintentionally and inevitably failed to include someone. So I can only hope that each of them knows the debt and gratitude that will be in my heart for as long as I live.

FINALLY, I WANT TO TRY TO ACKNOWLEDGE the love and appreciation that I feel, but can't adequately express in words, for my children, their spouses (who are like my own children), and my grandchildren: the Ullmans—Vivian, Jim, Alysa, Andrew, and Lindsay; the Simons—Leslie, Roger, Julie, Melissa, and Jessica; and the Kleins—Lynn, Jim, Jennifer, and Lexi. They have always been a source of great joy to their father/father-in-law/grandfather and me. In the nearly two years since we lost him, they have been the bedrock of strength and comfort on which I have relied every day. Several of them have helped in very practical ways to make this book a reality. But even more important, just as the person to whom this book is dedicated made it possible for me to find joy, laughter, and true happiness after the dark years of my enslavement, my family today has helped restore my faith in the wonder of life and love, even after incalculable and irretrievable loss.

I realize that these last two paragraphs about friends and family perhaps sound too perfect. But I write these thoughts for you, my readers, for a reason. Caring words and deeds are the light of life. Indeed, as has been wisely said, the light of just one candle can banish the darkness, and all the world's darkness cannot extinguish the light of just one candle. Tell someone today that you care.

Gerda Weissmann Klein
Scottsdale, Arizona

The Klein Family

Bread

*I*T WAS PROBABLY NOVEMBER. Though I am no longer sure, I do remember that there was a thick blanket of leaves on the ground. It was late afternoon. I was on my way to Loblaw's grocery store, quite in awe at the bounty of available goods and food—as I remain to this day. I still can't think of anything more satisfying than to buy fruit, vegetables, and meats; to bring them home in sturdy brown bags; and to stock the refrigerator and pantry shelves. But in those years long ago, going marketing was a veritable feast in itself. I would find reasons to visit the supermarket daily, even to get only one item.

Of course, I can't recall what was on my shopping list that particular day. A gusty wind was blowing, and grotesquely shaped clouds were sailing across the fall sky. I took a considerable amount of time in the supermarket, scrutinizing all the shelves, and was especially fascinated by the displays of canned food, whose brightly colored exteriors beckoned tantalizingly. Those labels became my sources of information. When they showed a picture of beans or plums, I knew what the contents would be and could take the can from the shelf without the embarrassment of having to ask for it in my halting English. Once I took the last yellow box of Velveeta cheese and felt guilty. I returned the next day to find to my joy and relief that the shelf had been fully replenished. Each shopping spree would thus help me to increase my vocabulary, I reasoned, and it was a worthwhile occupation in which I indulged every day. This system was not without some comical mix-ups, but by and large, it worked. Altogether I must have spent more than an hour in the store.

1

When I came out, it had turned dark, and snow was falling heavily. I hurried home, carrying my precious cargo. The wind mixed the swirling leaves with snow, whipping my face. My eyelashes were caked with it, and my feet felt wet and icy. Dashing into the house and up the stairs, I opened the door to my warm apartment, took off my shoes, and started to unpack the bag. Among the items was loaf of bread. A whole loaf of bread—mine! It brought back to mind the long years in the camps and the cold, wet, icy death march, when the unattainable dream became a loaf of bread, savored in a warm, secure place. I took the loaf into the living room with me. I sat near the window and watched the falling snow, swirling in the gales and gusts of wind to the earth below me. Above me more snow was coming endlessly from the leaden sky. In the safety of my dry, warm home, I sat watching the elements that could no longer harm me. I felt so rich! This was the moment I had dreamed about so often; this was the ultimate happiness! It had finally come to pass. But what was this curious anguish—why, then, was I not happy? I had never imagined that I would be able to feel this way once the war was over. Here I was, living safely in the United States, being loved and cared for by my husband in my own home, with an entire loaf of bread all to myself.

I thought of Ilse, Suse, Liesel, and all my friends in their shallow graves, frozen now and covered by fresh snow. When we dreamed of that loaf of bread, we had never given a thought to the fact that only a few of us would be destined to attain that dream. I had to eat that loaf of bread. I *had* to. But Ilse would have known, as would have Suse and all the hundreds I remembered. They would have understood what had driven me to this. So I kept eating the bread, watching the snow, and recalling the past. When I came to almost the end of the loaf, I noticed that it was soggy and tasted salty from my tears, but I gulped it down anyway.

Looking back now, I think that right then and there I laid the foundation for my life's work. I didn't understand it then, of course, for I lacked the detachment lent by time and distance and was far too shocked by my unhappiness. But I see now that the solution was so simple: To eat my loaf alone would never give me joy! Was it that night or a few days later that I told Kurt that I wanted to do some type of volunteer work? Surely there must be some organization here, helping those people who had remained in Europe in the DP camps.

Kurt was delighted and said he would inquire at the local Jewish community service office. He returned with the news that my help would be most welcome. Elated, I shared with Kurt's Aunt Therese the news that I was enlisting in this program as a volunteer. She listened to my exuberance and thought it was an excellent idea that I should think of working but gently implied that volunteer work was for the wealthy. I agreed. I was rich, wasn't I?

The Beverly Hills Hotel

LATE 1960s, BEVERLY HILLS, CALIFORNIA

*T*HE SUNSHINE INVADING MY ROOM WAS BRILLIANT AND SPARKLING. The sheets on my bed felt smooth and cool; the blanket, though feather light, was warm. I picked up the phone to order breakfast. In the thickly carpeted bathroom, the towels were enormous and thirsty. I inhaled the fragrance of the soap and turned on the shiny faucets, which emitted a forceful stream that filled the tub in minutes. I felt pampered, and—no question—I was.

Breakfast was wheeled in on a serving table with as much pomp and circumstance as I imagined might attend a display of the British crown jewels. A heavy damask cloth covered the table; the matching napkin was huge. The glass of orange juice nestled in an avalanche of crushed ice. The soft-boiled egg was cuddled and kept warm under a quilted cozy. The waiter inquired with the earnest demeanor of a major-domo whether four minutes' boiling time for the egg was to my liking. The toast reposed under a majestic silver dome. Each detail had been arranged with the utmost care and planning, down to the rosebud meticulously placed in a small vase on the tray. The morning paper, folded just right to fit the palm of my hand, lay to the left of the vase. Perfection.

The waiter departed, and I ate slowly, savoring each morsel, the fragrance of good, rich coffee filling the air. I decided to open the balcony door. I was eager for the warmth of the sun because back in Buffalo, New York, where I had just come from for my speaking engagement here, autumn had passed and winter was approaching rapidly.

4

A whiff of fragrant air greeted me as I slid the door open and stepped out. Below lay a profusion of green and blooming trees and shrubs in the orderly, yet wild disarray of a cultivated tropical paradise. Secluded and surrounded by pools and flowers were the bungalows of the Beverly Hills Hotel, still a playground of the rich and famous now, in the late 1960s. Liveried waiters, carrying food and flowers, moved to various doors; here and there gardeners could be seen at work.

The tree-lined avenue to my left, claimed to be the most beautiful street in the world, led to the palm-ringed hotel, which stood like a pink birthday cake surrounded by candles. Cars glided noiselessly to a halt in one fluid motion. Doors were opened by uniformed attendants. Beautiful, slender women and handsome, suntanned men alighted. The procession of Rolls-Royces, Jaguars, and Mercedes-Benzes disappeared into some vast underground parking area, waiting to be summoned again to convey the rich, the prominent, and the beautiful to other, similar destinations.

As I craned to look around the corner of my flower-trellised balcony, the newspaper I was holding dropped out of my hand. I bent to retrieve it and, in that moment, caught a glimpse of my reflection in the glass of the balcony door.

For an instant, it arrested the motion I was used to performing daily at home: the same stooping in order to get the *Buffalo Evening News*, which the paperboy delivers in the late afternoon.

In a flash, I saw the image of our suburban street, the porch, and the spot on which the paper usually lands, the crack in the cement where the stoop has settled a little.

It would be windy and gray in Buffalo and probably snowing lightly; the trees and bushes would be bare. The swirling wind would have littered the porch with broken twigs and bits of newspaper, blown over the steps toward the door.

Inside the hall would be the children's boots; the mat would be strewn with leaves amid rivulets of melting snow. The usual dishes from the children's snacks would no doubt be filling the sink. I could picture the open cupboards, the slight trail of sugar leading across the pantry, the schoolbooks scattered all around, along with a lone mitten and a lunchbox.

I could almost hear the ringing of the phone, almost picture the laundry basket heaped high at the basement door.

I turned around and looked at my elegant hotel room—the immaculate, orderly room—the bud vase, the gleaming silver, the heavy carpets, and the drapes that shut out all noise. So quiet, so sedate, so empty. I wished I were at home.

Coming to Buffalo

SEPTEMBER 13, 1946, BUFFALO, NEW YORK

I REMEMBER COMING TO BUFFALO. The trip on the swift *Empire State* took a mere eight hours from New York City all the way across the state. The train was streamlined, silver, and all the seats were occupied. As the afternoon wore on, I lazily dreamed about what Buffalo would be like. It would be tucked away far from the huge metropolis on some lofty plateau surrounded by trees. I had seen some movies of America; I can't recall if they were of the 1939 World's Fair. I envisioned, as I suppose most Europeans then did, the New World as tall, shiny, lofty, anchored somehow to an ever-sunny sky. The glimpse of Manhattan's skyscrapers had been awesome, but not satisfying. The rush and noise and tumult left me bewildered. Now I was truly coming home. Buffalo gleamed in my thoughts like an enchanted island, and the hum of the wheels on the tracks was singing a refrain: "I am coming home; I am coming home."

I saw myself floating up somehow to a tall chrome-and-glass city of tomorrow. Excitement started to mount as I realized that I would reach it that day. What would our apartment be like? Kurt said how terribly lucky we were that his friend Art had been able to secure one for us in the postwar housing shortage. It was on a lovely tree-shaded street not far from the famed Kleinhans Music Hall, Kurt said. I imagined large, airy rooms with huge windows, starkly modern, all conveniences concealed, but at the touch of a button, a door would open and reveal a kitchen, neat, bright, and shiny. I would be the mistress of a household, prepare fabulous meals, serve them on a flower-decked table, and wear my wonderful Paris creations. Even in Buffalo, I was sure they would be most fashionable.

Tonight, tonight I would be home. After seven long years, home again! The first home of my adulthood. My first home. The train pulled into the station and stopped. Buffalo. We had arrived. Art and his wife met us at the station. They spoke English, and I could not understand a word. Kurt was at home. We collected all our belongings and emerged from the immense hall of the station. I was going to see it now. I was about to have my first glimpse of my new home.

I looked to the skyline for the tall buildings of my dreams. There were none. The street on which we traveled was dimly lit. Nowhere were there the bright arches of light I had imagined, the multicolor of neon I had expected America to be. On both sides of the streets were squat wooden houses with porches, somehow reminiscent of the countryside in Czechoslovakia. Only those houses had not sat on wide lawns but close together, as if huddling for comfort.

My dreams had fled. Was I disappointed? Far from it! I was set on loving everything about my new home. I was ready to defend it even to myself. To this day, I find it annoying if a stranger criticizes Buffalo.

Looking at the darkened, somehow poor-looking streets that were suddenly so far from the Place de la Concorde and the brightness of the Rue de Rivoli, I thought how wonderful, how homey, how free of pretense my new home was. I would live there among those houses, which must be as comfortable as an old shoe. It would have been difficult to become a housewife in some ultramodern apartment. Scared of gadgets and mechanical things, I would never be able to master them. This, on the other hand, would be easy. This was really coming home.

We drove for quite a while. I tried in vain to catch some phrase and understand it. I understood a word here and there, either remembering from my English lessons or because it was similar to German, but they were talking too fast. Each sentence fled before I latched onto even one word. They were laughing and catching up. Every so often they would turn to me and say something in German, but I had no part in their conversation or in their lives. We came to a wide, tree-lined avenue and stopped in front of a stately three-floored house. It looked friendly and inviting. The broad front porch and the supporting columns were freshly painted white. The foyer was brightly lit and inviting. Kurt looked up and said in English, "Hey, this is a bit of all right!"

"Hold your horses," Art replied. I understood that, but I did not know what horses had to do with our new home. I always somehow get confused with horses. We had been given coupons in Paris. They had said "Cheval."

"What's that for?" I had asked Kurt.

"A horse."

"What about a horse?" I was used to obeying everything that smacked even slightly of the official: If you got a coupon, I thought, you *had* to buy what was on it. "What would we do with a horse?" I had inquired, somehow alarmed. Kurt laughed and explained that it was for horse meat, and that we didn't have to get any if we didn't want to. Now Art had lost me again with that new reference to horses.

We climbed to the third floor. After the second floor, the stairs were much narrower and steeper. The landing was not curved. A single suspended bulb lit the hall. The house, which had been a small mansion, was now converted into ten apartments. Ours was apartment number ten, formerly a part of the servants' quarters. The door swung open to reveal a linoleum floor, bright and friendly with pink and blue flowers. To the right was a living room painted apple green and furnished in what Kurt later called "early Goodwill." The bedroom was tiny, with a sloping ceiling and a single window looking out on an airshaft. But there on the crude, battered dresser stood a vase with the most beautiful red roses. The envelope read "Mrs. Klein." It was the first time I had been so addressed in English. Inside was a card. "Welcome home. All my love always. Kurt." It was in English, and I understood it. I understood with my brain and with my heart. I was home. Home! And as happy as I had dreamed I would be.

The place had possibilities, Art and Kurt had said. It could be fixed up and look really nice. I didn't care. All I knew was that when Art and his wife left, we would be alone. After they left and after Kurt had fallen asleep, I got out of bed and inspected my home. I opened every drawer in the kitchen. I opened and shut them, opened and shut them again. I let the water run from the faucets. Art had thoughtfully stocked the refrigerator with food. I opened it and took out an apple. It shut too quickly, the handle almost jerking from my hand. I was alarmed, frightened. What if . . .? And then, suddenly I was relieved. I was home! I was allowed to do that. How many, many years had it been since I had the freedom of taking something that belonged to me! It was all mine now: the apple *and* the refrigerator. I opened the door again fully intending to let it slam shut. Instead I caught it in time, closed it gently. I took the apple and walked into the bathroom, turning on the light. It was very bright. I looked into the mirror and saw a young woman's face, framed by dark hair. I was wearing a hand-embroidered white satin nightgown from one of the finest shops on the Place Vendôme. Behind me on the wall was a decal of morning glories garlanding toward the bathtub. I can still see the reflection of me as I was so many years ago. I still remember my expression of absolute bliss as I said to myself, I am home in Buffalo, New York. I am home in America. I am home in our apartment. I am eating my apple from my refrigerator. I ate the apple, core, pits, and all. I turned out the lights and crept into bed. Kurt's arm automatically went around me. "Thank you for bringing me home," I whispered. But he was asleep.

September 11

I SAW IT AGAIN AS I HAD IN COUNTLESS DREAMS. Not towers of fairy-tale castles, but huge, gleaming skyscrapers reaching to ever-blue skies, shimmering golden in the rays of the sun. My image of what was going to be my home: Buffalo, New York. The small wooden houses with dimly lighted porches were like refugees huddling together for closeness and warmth. Was I disappointed? Far from it! This was dear, familiar, comfortable. I would fit in, would belong, and would be truly at home. The vision of those proud, lofty, sunlit towers lodged in me as symbols of everything that was to be in my future. A family, a home, freedom, friends, new places. Maybe some as yet undefined work and glamour. It was all starting now. I was at home at last. Those gleaming towers could be tucked safely into my heart as cherished jewels. Now those crystalline towers, those bright many-faceted jewels, would house all that was to come. How could I have conceived in my limited imagination that my future reality would dwarf my keenest dreams? America! I fell in love with America the moment of my liberation, when I saw the white star of its army on the mud-spattered hood of a jeep. It was the brightest star I had ever seen. I shed my first tears of sorrow and joy in the arms of a man who wore the American uniform: my beloved Kurt.

America has given me everything. As a small child, I had been taught to pray, and that a prayer should be an expression of gratitude and never a supplication. My gratitude to America always outdistanced any criticism I might silently have felt.

ETCHED IN MY MIND FOREVER is the day I received my citizenship. I was pregnant with my first child. I had studied everything I could lay my hands on. Trembling, I stood in front of the judge. He asked: "What is the name of our president?"

"Harry S Truman*," I replied.

"Congratulations." He shook my hand.

That was all? I wished he had asked me what the S stood for. He did not. That was all. I was dizzy with awe and joy. My baby stirred within me. "We belong; we are both Americans."

I SAT MUTE, TRANSFIXED. Gazing at the screen, seeing the towers, anchored to the ever-blue sky, *struck*. Fire, smoke, walls like protective hands around a bleeding heart, slipping, helplessly gliding into an abyss. The towers, the bright jewel of my fulfillment, my America, mortally wounded. The sun shone, and the sky was blue. Weeping, Kurt held me in his arms. It was September 11, 2001.

We had arrived at National Airport in Washington, D.C., on one of the last flights on September 10 for several appointments and meetings. Later, as I looked at the scenes of devastation on September 11, I knew without any doubt that all the people in this country, no matter where they were, no matter how glamorous and luxurious their surroundings, wanted nothing more than to be with their own families, sharing a boring evening at home.

SUDDENLY I WAS BACK. Back on another September day, Sunday, September 3, 1939, at 9:10 in the morning, when the first German motorcycle roared down the road in front of my home. I was fifteen. That glorious, rich

---

* The letter "S" stood for the names of both of Truman's grandfathers. So as not to play favorites, he simply used the initial "S," omitting the period.

autumn day, with flowers bright in my garden, with my parents and brother inside the safe walls of my childhood home, marked the destruction of all I knew and loved. The murder of my parents and brother would follow. I became a number. I had no home, no family, no country, no identity. My life and death were at the whim of a bitter enemy. My father, who until then had had the ultimate power to grant or deny my wishes, was as help-less as me. Now, here in Washington, the seat of great power, I saw the bewilderment and fear in the faces of people as I had seen them so many Septembers ago. The same haunting questions: "How could this happen? What next?" Frantically we called our children and grandchildren. Four of our granddaughters were in Washington. I tried to reassure them, but could not. I was always the optimist in the family. Kurt was more cautious and more pragmatic. Suddenly our roles switched. Or did he do it for me? "It is terrible," he kept repeating, "but this is America."

"But we are Jewish," I would reply.

"Yes, we are, and we are Americans. This is not Germany. This is America, thank God."

The hours became days, and the days became weeks. The nights held fearful demons of the past invading my dreams, but the reality, despite all fears, was bright and the memories brighter. The births of our chil-dren. Their first day of school. The Fourth of July and unfurling, with joy, the American flag. It snapped in the wind while the children laughed and played. Yes, the flag flying from our home. Can an American who has never been deprived of freedom understand? I saw the swastika fly-ing over my childhood home, its poisonous spider reaching out to strangle us. But the Stars and Stripes had always seemed to shield and protect our children and home. And now as America was under attack, memo-ries of what this country has meant to me came flowing back.

THE EMERALD LUSH, GENTLE HILLS OF BEAUTIFUL NORMANDY kissing the blue of the sea. Colleville-sur-Mer. The American Cemetery, its perfect rows of white marble crosses spreading a sea of sadness across the rolling hillside. An occasional Star of David among the rows. Thousands and thousands who never came home.* The bronze statue is edged with the words "Spirit of American Youth." Omaha Beach. Pointe du Hoc. The Ranger Memorial. Utah Beach. Kurt landed here on D-Day plus 10 or so. We sat on the beach on Yom Kippur and lit memorial candles in the sand for his friends who died there. We held each other's hands, his thoughts, I am sure, going back to those hours when he landed here as a young man. My thoughts reflected on our synagogue at home, and people praying. The holiness of the sanctuary of Normandy Beach, with its gently rippling waves that kissed the shore, somehow connected me to some unfathomable sadness and unwarranted hope. When much, much later I read Plato's words: "Only the dead have seen the end of war," I remembered Utah Beach and my feelings there.

I am Jewish and I am American. "Why do you feel so passionately about Israel when you are so fiercely American?" I have been asked countless times. In response I have tried to explain that I don't have the privilege of looking back with love at a country I can claim as my own. My love for Israel is the love I hold for my parents and brother, and loving Israel is a way for me to honor their memory. My love for America is the love I hold for my husband, children, and grandchildren. There is no conflict in that love, for you cannot be a loving wife or mother without having been a devoted daughter first.

America had given me the most endearing and valuable gift of acceptance of honoring my religion, where in the past I got nothing but derision, insults, and a branding with shame and unworthiness.

How can I describe my awe and gratitude when Kurt and I were invited to the dedication of the Jewish Chapel at West Point? We watched as the Torah, our holy scriptures, was greeted by a fife-and-drum corps of cadets of all races. Cadets wearing yarmulkes (head coverings) escorted

---

* Facing the graves as if in embrace is a white, pillared semi-circle upon which are these words: "This embattled shore, portal of freedom, will be forever hallowed by the ideals, the valor, and the sacrifices of our fellow countrymen."

the Torah into the chapel and placed it under the chuppah, the traditional Jewish marriage canopy. The general in charge spoke movingly of
the Bible and the Ten Commandments, which the Jews gave the world.
To me, having seen the Torah burned and trampled on, to see it honored
by men and women in the uniforms of my liberators and symbolically
wedded to West Point was an extraordinary moment.

APRIL DRESSES WASHINGTON IN THE GLORY OF SPRING. The city is a breathtaking bouquet of color and fragrance. But on that particular April day in
1993, it was not the shower of cherry blossoms descending from a cloudless blue sky. Angry, swift-moving dark clouds sent a bitter cold shower
of snowflakes, freezing the heart of the blossoms of spring. Around the
corner from the graceful Jefferson Memorial and other white marble
shrines to freedom is a museum of granite, red brick, and steel that tells
the grim story of what happens when democracy and decency collapse.
Braving the gusty icy wind, President Clinton, Israeli President Chaim
Herzog, with scores of other heads of state and clergy, sat outside the
United States Holocaust Memorial Museum. There stood the American
president. My president with leaders of other governments, heads bowed
in reverence at this holy shrine dedicated to the memory of our family
and those like them, who died because of the hatred of oppressors.

Some eight years later the museum was our principal reason for being in Washington on September 11, 2001. We were to attend a meeting
of its governing council, of which I was privileged to be a member.

The brutal face of hate rose from the collapse of the Twin Towers,
stripping me of the fragile skin of my security, of the blessed present,
and instead infusing in me fear of my known past and the hope for my
family's and my country's future. "This is America," Kurt was saying,
holding me in his arms. "We have been wounded, but this is different.
This is America." On the steps of the Capitol they gathered: Americans;
all races, all religions, all colors, and all political persuasions. As Win-
ston Churchill said, quoting Bourke Cochran, the famous Irish-
American orator and statesman: "In a society where there is democratic

tolerance and freedom under the law, many kinds of evils will crop up, but give them a little time and they usually breed their own cure." And Churchill added: "I do not see any reason to doubt the truth of that. There is no country in the world where the process of self-criticism and self-correction is more active than in the United States." America has given me everything I hold dear. America has never taken anything from me that I loved. Even Kurt, my most beloved being on earth, was taken from me on an April day, but not on American soil.

It was Friday, August 3, 2001. A bright glorious day at the U.S. Naval Academy in Annapolis, Maryland. To me any centralized military place seems sinister and frightening. In fact, neither West Point nor Annapolis is. They exude safety, awe-inspiring grandeur, and majesty. It was the fifth time in as many years that Kurt and I stepped to the podium, and twelve hundred plebes rose to attention. Confronting this sea of young people, all attired in dazzling white, my heart swelled with pride and gratitude as I listened to Kurt addressing this incoming class of future naval officers. This is the conclusion of what he said that day:

> *Each generation faces its own challenges and must deal with them as circumstances dictate. I cannot tell you what events or developments you will face in times to come, but I can tell you that there are lessons to be learned from past history. For my generation, the issues were clear-cut. We had to stop unprecedented evil from spreading and subjugating all those in this world whom these fanatics' ideology considered inferior and, therefore, not entitled to exist, in direct contrast to what we in this country regard as our inalienable rights. My generation felt privileged to serve this country in its time of need. In retrospect, what I hear whenever I meet some of my erstwhile comrades-in-arms are these overriding sentiments: a pride to have served our country, gratitude for having come through those events that molded us and defined us as the persons we were yet to be, and an awareness of how fortunate*

we and our families are to be able to live the values we so ardently defended and preserved. You have chosen a career of service to your country and taken on the responsibility of leadership. In this new century, you will be on the cutting edge of many decisions that will irrevocably affect the outcome of history. I can only express my profound thanks to you for safeguarding all that is precious to us in this way of life that we cherish. In all that lies ahead, I wish you the rewards and satisfaction that are sure to be yours for the career you have chosen and the benefits it will bring for you and for us all. More than anything, I wish you a time of peace—and Godspeed to you!

Thirty-nine days later was September 11.

Niagara Falls

*A*UTUMN. The sky, the clouds, the wind, the rustle of leaves underfoot. Pumpkins and apple cider. For me they all evoke a string of memories of my first change of seasons in Buffalo and of my first Thanksgiving in this country. The surface meaning of the holiday was easy to understand. But the implications were to be brought home to me in a forceful and unexpected way—and not on the day itself.

That weekend I was going to have a second and more leisurely look at Niagara Falls. Kurt and I would be in the company of another couple: Kurt's oldest and closest friend, Art, and his wife. They were to pick us up for the drive to the falls, where we were to meet yet another couple. All were friends of long standing. Our plans called for sightseeing and then dinner at the Hotel Niagara.

For the first time since my arrival in the United States a few weeks before, I found I was gaining familiarity with the language. Thus far it had been mostly a babble of voices from which an occasional recognizable word would surface, but whose exact meaning within the larger context would usually elude me. Now it seemed that I understood the gist of conversations, although some words were still strange to me. Sporadically, I would even venture a halting comment in English.

I was particularly curious about what my second impression of the falls would be. Although I had not admitted it, my first, hurried view of this great natural wonder, though I found it grand enough, had left me feeling slightly let down. Because of the images retained from my school days in Poland, I had conjured up visions of monumental scope.

18

Of course, the war years had blurred such recollections, but my expectations in those postwar days still ran on the assumption that everything in the United States—and that included mighty Niagara—was simply colossal and beyond imagination. The fact was, that autumn I was still taking the measure of my new environment, in the dual role of recent bride and new arrival in a totally strange and different country.

The grandeur of the United States, as much as its plethora of unrationed goods, continually amazed me. And my second look at the falls confirmed my early expectations after all: It *was* overwhelmingly spectacular!

When we got to the hotel, we found that the other couple had secured an excellent table and the restaurant was filling up rapidly. Adjacent tables were being taken, and a warm, congenial atmosphere prevailed. I was beginning to feel much more at ease with Kurt's friends now that I could communicate after a fashion. It had been a perfect day, and I felt supremely happy.

Relishes and warm rolls appeared on our table. I was only too aware that such a meal would have been unthinkable for me just a while before. Course after course appeared. Wine was served. Glasses were raised, toasting our marriage and my recent arrival. At one point, Art stood up and indicated that a speech was in order. I felt no small amount of embarrassment.

Heads were turning, and it was evident that our group was becoming the focus of attention. Oh well, I thought, he is an attorney—he must enjoy that sort of thing.

He spoke slowly, and I understood most of what he was saying. And then, after a few sentences, one of his phrases ran through me like an electric shock. Why, could this be?—I must be mistaken! My English wasn't good enough after all. He couldn't be saying what I thought I was hearing: ". . . and in my opinion, President Truman is a fool and an idiot!"

I grasped Kurt's arm. "Stop him! Stop him! Don't let him do that!" I pleaded.

Everyone else at our table wore a self-conscious grin, but I was trembling with fear and agitation.

Art, quickly becoming aware of my anguish, leaned over, patted me on the head, and said, with a completely calm voice: "Don't worry, nothing will happen. I made that statement for your benefit. The Gestapo won't come. No one will arrest me."

Then he directed his voice to the curious faces in the vicinity.

"Just in case you're wondering; this young lady is new to our shores," he said, "and I wanted to show her what freedom of speech really means."

But it wasn't that simple for me.

That night I woke up several times. The evening's events kept going around and around in my head, and they left me deeply disturbed. The following evening I casually asked Kurt about some matter I knew would result in his having to call Art.

Then I held my breath while the connection was made. For me the wait was interminable, but Kurt was completely unperturbed. I moved closer, and after what seemed an eternity, I could hear the resonant voice answering on the other end.

The two friends talked as they always did, punctuating the conversation with laughter and easy banter. Afterward Kurt gave me a matter-of-fact account of the conversation.

He never suspected for a moment that I had engineered the call because I wanted him to contact Art. All assurances about freedom of speech notwithstanding, I had been afraid—afraid for Art after his extraordinary behavior. Art is gone now. We miss him very much. His theatrics that day long ago in Niagara Falls were to be the first of many displays that were frequently outrageous and usually very funny. But throughout many years of friendship we most cherished his enormous devotion and generosity. In years since, when I have had occasion to take visitors to Niagara Falls, I usually contrive to make a detour that will take me past the old Hotel Niagara. To me it is as symbolic as the Washington Monument and the Lincoln Memorial. It was my first understanding of freedom of speech.

New Year's Eve

*W*E WERE GOING TO HAVE A PARTY, our very first newlyweds' party, a big party to celebrate New Year's! My excitement knew no bounds, and we talked of nothing else. I started to bake and prepare with the help of Kurt's Aunt Therese, who taught me to convert measurements from pounds to cups and lent me all kinds of utensils, decorative jars, and bowls that would turn our party into a success. I went again and again to food stores as well as to my all-time favorite, the "five-and-ten."

I suppose I was sufficiently childlike and naive to revel in the delights the store offered. Aside from not having had a normal growing-up, when one's senses of style and taste develop, I had been starved of brightness and tinsel because of the years of wartime austerity and deprivation. Woolworth's fire-engine-red sign with gold lettering beckoned, offering an abundance of available goods—things I had not seen in years or had never seen before. Best of all, they were within my financial reach. I think it may be difficult to understand what it was like to come from the darkness and hunger of war-torn Europe. There had been a stopover in Paris, where beautiful luxury items were alluringly displayed. Although expensive beyond belief, some of them had been made available to me through my uncle's generosity. But they were too good, too precious, too irreplaceable. And I found it difficult to reconcile them with myself and my everyday life. Using them seemed akin to wearing a diamond tiara when cooking hot dogs.

Here was America with all its bounty, and I was part of it. The trip to Woolworth's usually resulted in a myriad of little items I would discover each day. I reveled in the extraordinary range of shapes and colors. Often I saw something ornamental and fancy I had wanted as a child, when I needed parental approval for the expenditure. Now I was able to buy such things at random. I bought an enormous box of Snow Caps nonpareils, brought them home, and ate them all up. To my great delight, I also found multicolored balloons. Kurt said they were a must for a New Year's party. I had such a hard time selecting colors and shapes of balloons that I decided to get *all* colors and *all* shapes. So I splurged on fifty of them, which must have cost me all of fifty cents. But it was worth it. Next came quantities of confetti and streamers. I kept all the party treasures in a special box, which I would look at several times a day. One day I found a store that was disposing of an enormous box of a white substance that had been used as artificial snow for window displays. Apparently they had overstocked or were merely getting ready for spring and summer displays. I still couldn't get used to the fact that anybody would throw anything out. Just a few months ago in Europe, if you needed anything, you had to bring along a document entitling you to replace the precious original commodity. Once when I went to a hairdresser, I had to bring along not only a towel, shampoo, and soap, but a piece of coal to contribute to the heating of the water.

Now, here, someone was throwing out a perfectly usable item, and I couldn't resist availing myself of someone else's careless disposal. And so I lugged the box home, but was initially at a loss as to what to do with it. Showing my "loot" to Kurt that evening, we both hit on a brilliant idea. At midnight we would create a snowstorm in our living room. The alcove had a dormer on the window side. That part sloped down to a low point from the ceiling. With some difficulty, we affixed a crepe-paper ceiling below that point and filled the empty "loft" with the artificial snow. Though it billowed and balked at some points, it held. Contriving a story to lure our guests into the alcove before midnight and stick their hands out the window, we hoped to make them part of an old European New Year's custom for good luck. At midnight we would pull the string, releasing the avalanche of snow and good fortune.

The best part of our party was the guest list, for it was no guest list at all. Every day Kurt was on the phone, trying to determine who was back home. One call would lead to another and then to another. As he tried to explain to me who those friends were, he would exclaim in delight when he reached them or their parents in his ceaseless pursuit to track them down. Most of them had just arrived back in town after their military service. And they promised to come to the party, every one of them. Even if they had prior plans, they would try to come, and bring their wives or girlfriends. They would come if only to have a drink, but they would come. Now the question arose: What should I prepare, and how much? I was worried, but Kurt laughed. People here are different; you'll see. This is just an informal New Year's party with the boys back from overseas. Have cold cuts and potato salad and nuts and lots of drinks; it will be great. We broke into the meager remains of our savings in order to throw the greatest party ever. I think it came to the colossal amount of twenty-seven dollars. But it actually turned out to be the greatest party ever!

THE BIG DAY CAME. The apartment was decorated and in readiness. Aunt Theresa had lent me glasses and all kinds of trays and bowls. Kurt brought me flowers, and I am sure that no hostess could have felt greater pride at her gatherings than what I felt when I surveyed the preparations for my first party. I dressed in a splendid ballgown. It consisted of my exquisite white satin Paris nightgown, which was sleeveless and cut along straight lines. I had taken down our new white living-room curtains to make room for the false ceiling-snow contraption. I looped these over a satin belt at my waist, thus creating an enormous crinoline skirt. It looked spectacular.

As the guests were arriving, there were shrieks of delight and laughter. With each new arrival, there was more hugging and boisterous reunions. Some of the men were still in uniform. This was a brave new world. Happy New Year! I caught phrases: "Good to be home; so good to be home." "That's what we dreamed of in the Philippines, in the foxholes in France." "Happy New Year! Let's drink to peace!" I was introduced, and they came around to kiss the bride. I was so happy. I had never been so happy before. I felt I knew those men; they had liberated me. Their uniforms were dear to me. Symbols of freedom. I loved them. They had fought and slain the monster. They had made the world safe, free, and beautiful. I was so grateful to them, my heroes, my friends. They were my family now. I was a part of them. For the first time in my life I was a part of a winning team. "C'mon, let's drink to peace! This is the end of all wars! Happy New Year!"

What plans they had; all seemed to see unlimited horizons before them. Some were going to college, thanks to Uncle Sam. One had just become engaged and would marry in June. "Yeah! Drink to that!" There were stories of narrow escapes in the Pacific and in other parts of the world. "Yeah! I never thought I would be back home with friends on New Year's Eve. Let's drink to that!" Some were hunting for apartments, and Art was soon surrounded by eager apartment searchers. Someone was going into his "old man's business," but just for a while, you understand. "I didn't fight a war in Europe to go into my old man's shop. No, sir. I'm looking around, but I'll give the old man a hand in the meantime." I understood almost all the remarks by now, and what I did not understand, I somehow sensed. They were in my home, but I was *at* home with all of them. I wanted to hug and kiss all those young men and women, to thank them for making me a part of them. I wanted to shout, "Hooray!" although I would never have dared. It was the sort of atmosphere in which one wanted to take off one's hat and cheer. There was a camaraderie and an esprit de corps you find only during extraordinary times.

Suddenly, there was a loud knock on the door. My heart skipped a beat. Oh God, was it all a dream? Had my bubble burst? I ran to the door. There stood a very handsome young man, the drink in his hand splashing back and forth. He was mumbling something about our being noisy. At this point, Kurt appeared. The young man dropped his glass as they hugged and cheered. It turned out that he had been a friend of Kurt's before the war, in which he fought gallantly, and had returned a much-decorated hero. He had just gotten into town and was attending a party given by a friend of his in a borrowed apartment below ours. Now the floodgates burst open. There was much milling around, and it turned into a progressive party between the two apartments. Pandemonium broke out. At midnight we had our little practical joke, and the snow drifted onto the heads of the assembled guests. The party reached its zenith, and the momentum kept it going until all hours of the morning.

The cakes were decorated with the figures 1947 spelled out in tiny silver and gold candles. They beckoned brightly with the promise of the new year. My first year of marriage, my first year of freedom. My first year in America! The boys were back from the war they had fought, the world was free, and I was home again, all dreams fulfilled.

I looked out the partly opened window. It was snowing lightly. Gusts of snow hit my bare arms. I shivered for a moment, remembering the camps and the death march. A group of people emerged from the house across the street amid blowing horns and rattling noisemakers. I heard their voices. A friend of my husband's came up to me and, putting his arm around me, said, "Happy New Year. This is the greatest party, the happiest New Year."

I replied slowly in my very careful English, "Yes, the happiest New Year ever."

IT WAS THE HAPPIEST NEW YEAR'S EVE; and looking back, I think I understand why. I also understand why I have never liked New Year's since then and, lately, have begun to loathe the celebrations. On New Year's Eve in 1947, I was able to look back on all the tragedy and loss of the past years. I had nothing. I had lost everything but my life. I foresaw a year of total gain—a husband I adored, a country I loved, new friends, a new life. In the intervening years, I have been privileged to keep on gaining more and more. That made me uneasy because, with each gain there is always the fear of loss, and at New Year's, the celebration always turned into a prayer: May next year be as happy and full as the last one was. Ever since, I have always been reluctant to let the old year go. But 1947 opened with much promise.

The Bookcase

DECEMBER 1946

$\mathcal{W}$E RECEIVED ONE REALLY REGAL WEDDING GIFT when we were married: a check for thirty dollars. It gave rise to a long discussion. Should we do the prudent thing and exercise thrift, or should we throw caution to the winds and spend it all on something we desperately wanted?

Naturally we opted for the latter. And after that the choice was easy. Our indulgence would be a bookcase. Not an ordinary bookcase, of course, but a beautiful one, to house our prized literary possessions as well as our growing collection of 78 records.

After an exhaustive but fruitless search through several stores that sold new and used furniture, we hit on the bright idea of trying various carpentry shops.

And we finally found the right shop—one whose owner still seemed to be a craftsman of the old school. He agreed to build a piece of furniture to our specifications.

The bottom shelf would be wide enough for the record albums, the upper shelves narrower for books; the left end would be circular to serve as a base for a display of bric-a-brac. It would take all of our windfall to accomplish this, but we were heartened by the fact that we would have something special, something to be proud of, something to last a lifetime.

Having obviously found the right man for the job, we only reluctantly curbed our impatience during the five weeks it took until our masterpiece was completed.

It arrived one rainy late fall afternoon. At first I was taken aback,

26

almost disappointed, for I had imagined it would be stained dark to bring out the natural beauty of the wood grain. It seemed we had neglected to discuss that aspect of it, and it turned out to be made of bright, blond, highly varnished wood. Notwithstanding that, I fell in love with it.

Enthusiastically, I began to arrange our prized treasures, completely oblivious to the world around me. That's where Kurt found me when he got back from work. We forgot about dinner for a while, and instead labored mightily until the job was done to our satisfaction. The record albums were now in alphabetical order according to composer's last names, and we just couldn't get enough of looking at the gleaming gold-stamped spines of our small library, neatly arranged next to the shining wood.

The crowning achievement came with the placement of another proud acquisition: a brass-based lamp with a bright coral burlap shade. The base of the lamp, moreover, served as a planter for strands of trailing ivy. We moved the lamp this way and that, and nothing satisfied us until we settled for a spot just to the right of the circular section. As a final touch, I placed two figurines of glazed chartreuse pottery directly in front of the lamp.

One represented a giraffe, standing precariously on very long legs and craning its head toward the lamp. Next to it, in the circle of light, reposed a smaller doe. I arranged the ivy so that it enveloped the two small animals.

In the end, we stood back to admire our small gem of interior design, returning several times during and after dinner to give vent to our pride in this new possession.

Later that evening we went for a walk; prudently, as always, we turned off most of the lights, but this time we permitted ourselves the luxury of leaving the light on in the brass lamp. When we returned, much earlier than usual, we were filled with the anticipation of feasting our eyes anew. And there it was, bathed in the warm glow of the lamp, alive with the budding new ivy leaves.

Mercifully, the heavy horsehair "parlor chairs," as the landlord called them, were relegated to the shadows. Our bookcase with the gold-tooled spines of books and records reposed serenely—a hint of ever so many other, equally exciting acquisitions that the future would hold.

FEW IF ANY MATERIAL POSSESSIONS have given me the same soaring joy as did that bookcase. It has accompanied us along the convoluted paths of our life's journey.

It went to the apartment to which we "moved up," and subsequently, it graced the living room of our brand new home, which would have been bare, indeed, had it not been for our early foresight. We did replace the red shade eventually with a tooled-leather one. In time, as we acquired the standard accoutrements of a growing household, the bookcase inevitably had to give way to more refined tastes fostered by the production and sophistication this shining postwar world provided in ever-increasing measure.

But the position to which it was relegated was an honorable one. Our girls needed a place for their "dolls of all nations" collection. So the bookcase was painted white to match their room. Then, some years later, it went to our son's room to house his collection of trucks and cars. There it did yeoman service in chocolate brown and orange.

The day came when the car collection was put aside to make room for far more sophisticated gadgetry, and the bookcase wound up in another spot, in the upstairs hall. Once again it served to hold books and magazines. But the space was narrow, and it was forever in the way of running children. One day I stubbed my toe on it so badly that I hobbled around for days.

I should really throw that confounded nuisance out, I thought, but in my heart I knew I never would.

So it stands in the basement now, still holding an overflow of books. In a recent flood, it was badly damaged, and its paint has started to peel, revealing all the layers underneath. I need it, though, to stub my toe on from time to time when I run too fast.

It's not good to run too fast. When we run too fast, we tend to forget.

April 29

1958, BUFFALO, NEW YORK
ADDITIONAL REFLECTIONS: 1997, BOSTON, MASSACHUSETTS;
2001, SCOTTSDALE, ARIZONA

I CROSSED THE CHORES OFF MY REMINDER LIST, which for once I had not left at home. So far, so good. I had dropped off the dry cleaning, got the prescription from the drugstore, quickly found all the grocery items I was looking for, and was pleasantly surprised at the low price for imported peaches. I had also acquired a huge bunch of daffodils, always harbingers of spring for me, even during these unseasonably high Arizona temperatures, which seemed more like summer. Only three more items were on the agenda for the morning: get my hair done, return books to the library, and mail letters, some in need of additional postage.

My hair done, I felt relaxed and tidy. I pulled out my checkbook and automatically inquired, "What's today's date, Linda?"

Sweeping up the accumulated hair on the floor, she replied, "April twenty-ninth." Slowly I wrote out the date.

Ilse, forgive me, please forgive me for forgetting! I just had my hair washed, cut, and blow-dried; I shopped for food, got fresh peaches that were on sale, bought bread. More than half a century ago, there was another April 29. That was in 1945, and it was a bitter day, your last on this earth, and you must know that I remembered its every anniversary until now. Ilse, oh, Ilse, how I remember you!

I HAD KNOWN ILSE SINCE OUR EARLY CHILDHOOD DAYS in Bielitz/Bielsko, the town on the Polish/Czech border where we were born. She was a quiet child, introspective and withdrawn, whereas I was much more extroverted, given to babbling away for hours. When spoken to by adults, she had a tendency to cast her eyes to the ground. Her loveliest features were long silky eyelashes that imparted a piquant look to her face. It never failed to startle me to see her look up, for her eyes were always blazing with an unexpected fire.

Ilse was an extraordinarily gifted pianist and was accepted by the Vienna Academy of Music at a young age. Alas, after the Anschluss, she could no longer pursue those studies and returned home. That is when we became very close. At the time I was fifteen, and Ilse was my junior by nearly two years. Soon war came, and we were forced to live in the Jewish ghetto that had been established by the German occupiers, and from then on we saw each other daily. Ultimately, in June 1942, there was a day of separation from our families, our parents being deported to Auschwitz. Then German industrialists paid the authorities a nominal "handling fee" to acquire us as slave laborers to aid the German war effort. In the textile mills, and later in concentration camps, we were forever taken as sisters. It always came as a surprise to others to learn that we were not.

IN A SENSE, HOWEVER, WE DID BECOME FAMILY TO EACH OTHER—the only family either of us had. Over the ensuing three long years, we became inseparable and, near the end of a horror-filled, senseless death march, she died in my arms in a cold, windswept meadow in Czechoslovakia. She was eighteen. Her last words to a mercilessly cruel and hostile world were, "I am angry at no one, and I hope no one is angry at me." In her dying moments, she extracted a promise from me that I would try to hang on to life for one more week. A week later, perhaps at the very hour of her death, we were liberated by American troops.

That is why Ilse and that date in April are inextricably linked in my mind with the liberation she was not privileged to see. So much was she a part of my life that I feel I left something of myself in that nameless place in Czechoslovakia, under a tree that shelters Ilse's unmarked grave. She is often in my thoughts, but especially when April 29 comes around. Inevitable reminders keep me from my usual pursuits, and I let memory take over.

There is so much I remember about Ilse: her piano playing, her shy smile, tears trickling from under her long lashes. Curiously, I never thought of her as a friend; we never spoke about things friends usually discuss. To me she was just family, the sister I never had. Just as I was the little sister to my older brother, whom I adored, I now became an older sister to Ilse, who herself was an older sister to *her* sibling, Kitty. In her own manner, she looked up to me, made me feel important.

Although I remember countless details about her, memory fails me when it comes to the place where she died. What is particularly vexing is that I distinctly recall having seen the name of a nearby town on a signpost. Sometimes I think that some psychological trick of memory has erased it from my mind. I've often wondered whether the name of the village, had I retained it, would have allowed me to put Ilse to rest under the tree that must by now have grown mightily. But then, perhaps it was felled years ago to make room for a house where children now play on the site of Ilse's grave.

Because I strain to remember the spot, she is always with me, a constant reminder of everything we shared. She serves as my alter ego, my own young girlhood, but she, cast by fate to remain in that nameless place, was cheated of all that was to be mine.

Over the decades, I might have forgotten the date during the early hours of the morning, but the day would never pass without that particular memory coming back, leading me to reflect, to think of all I had been given and all that she had lost.

IN APRIL 1973, SPRING CAME EARLY TO WESTERN NEW YORK. There were buds on the trees in front of my home in Buffalo. They were of a very special, vulnerable, tender young shade of green. Bright strings of daffodils lined the emerald green approaches to a country club where I was attending a bridal shower. Bouquets of spring flowers formed the centerpieces of round tables, swathed in pink tablecloths. The chatter of guests over the lilting romantic music, the glow of radiant happiness on the face of the bride, my daughter Leslie, appeared to underscore the joy of the occasion. I saw my daughters break out in giggles.

I looked at them with different eyes, both my daughters.* A bridal shower on April 29, and I am the mother of the bride! Ilse, I thought of you that day!

ANOTHER APRIL 29 LEAPS TO THE FOREFRONT OF MY MIND. My son, Jimmy, was five years old, considerably younger than his two daughters are today. I had been the speaker at a meeting the evening before in Pittsburgh. The meeting over, I learned that my flight back to Buffalo had been canceled. I had promised my little son that I would be present at a performance of his kindergarten play the following morning. After some inquiries, it turned out that there was a bus leaving during the night. My hosts used all their powers of persuasion to sway me from my decision of taking a bus at three A.M., but, needless to say, I *had* to go. So I rode through the night until daybreak and, between fitful sleep, saw images of the dawn of another April 29 that Ilse never lived to see. I pictured the desolation and loneliness, the irony of seeing trees on the verge of bursting into bloom, heralding a spring Ilse would not witness.

By the time I reached Buffalo, my eyes were bloodshot and heavy from lack of sleep. All the same, I immediately proceeded to the already darkened school auditorium, where the performance had just begun. Scattered around the stage were children, chanting something about spring being here, some of them lisping, as kindergartners are wont to do. They were hopping around in their sneakers, a teacher laboring mightily to get them to stay in step. Just then I spotted Jimmy, separating

---

* Leslie, whose Hebrew name is Ilse's, was whispering to her older sister, Vivian Elissa. Vivian Elissa's initials—VE—signified VE Day, the day on which I met their father.

himself from the group and making his way to center stage through a group of little girls in party dresses. He made it through his part, took a bow, then scanned the front rows, which had been reserved for parents. Once he spotted me, his face broke into a huge grin. His brief moment in the limelight over, he dutifully took his place among a group of his classmates. Just then one little boy on the stage tripped over his shoelaces, stumbled, and promptly fell down, bringing another boy with him. A teacher scrambled to restore order while the chorus chanted lustily about the coming of spring.

I watched that scene through misty eyes and mused. Ilse had been angry at no one, but now I was angry on her behalf. She never knew the joy of such a moment. She would have *walked* from Pittsburgh, blessing every mile, if that privilege had been hers.

Each April 29 my heart fills with renewed pain and a sense of loss, for her and the millions like her who were deprived of the simplest joys of living.

STILL FURTHER BACK IN TIME, my two young girls had the measles, and the baby was running a temperature. After a mostly sleepless night, I went downstairs to the basement, ready to do a mountain of laundry, only to find the basement flooded from heavy rains that had come down during the night. Turning on the washing machine, all I could hear was a persistent hum. "Oh, God, this is going to be one of those days," I moaned.

Being radio-dispatched (a marvelous innovation in those days), the repairman from the appliance store where we had purchased the machine responded promptly to my call for help. He looked at the obstreperous machine that stood amid the puddles and, after fiddling with this knob and that, pronounced it beyond repair. Now would be an especially good time to get a new one, he emphasized, adding that there was a sale going on at the store from which he was dispatched. If I bought a new machine during their jubilee week, the service call would be deducted from the purchase price. He whipped out a service bill, jotting down the dates of the sale, April 29 to May 6.

Once he left, I stood in the damp basement, staring at the dates he had marked in red ink on a yellow slip. Ilse, please forgive me, forgive me for calling it "one of those days." What would you have given to have a home with a flooded basement, a broken washing machine, and three cranky children upstairs? Forgive me, Ilse, forgive me. If I buy a new washing machine this particular week, I will not have to pay for a service call. What a special deal! You once gave me a special deal, Ilse, pleading with me to hang on for one more week. I never could have imagined how good that deal would turn out for me.

By evening, the rain finally let up, and I decided to go in search of a washing machine. Kurt would stay with the children, trying to finish some necessary paperwork for the office. Approaching the store, I parked near the fence. Then, while I made my way to the entrance, several cars passed and splashed me. I felt wet, dirty, and bedraggled. The escalator took me to the basement, where the appliance section was located. Once downstairs, everything seemed bright, possibly due to the reflection of all the gleaming white and shiny chrome that was everywhere around me. There were towering refrigerators that appeared to be eyeing me arrogantly, and I quickly walked away, keeping my eyes open for washing machines. When I neared the back of the store, I spotted garish pink-and-yellow banners suspended from the ceiling that proclaimed: JUBILEE WEEK APRIL 29 TO MAY 6 SPECIAL SALE GET OUR BEST BUYS! The huge letters, bordered by silver tinsel, seemed to mock me.

My face must have reflected confusion, for surely I was upset, leaning on one of the washing machines. My old raincoat was half buttoned, wet, and smudged; a scarf was carelessly thrown around my head. I had probably neglected to put on lipstick before leaving the house. A young salesman was eyeing me, assessing whether it would be worth his while to try his pitch on me. I could see his reasoning: Not a very promising prospect, one of those women who shop without making up their mind. They usually can't afford it and wind up not buying.

Maybe this isn't the right day; I really ought to go home, I thought, and turned to leave. The salesman must have decided to try his luck all the same, this being a slow time on account of the rain. He would give it a try against his better judgment. And I was wishing there were a way of avoiding him. Besides, I wasn't fond of people who were too neatly dressed, wearing loud ties, whose hair was so neatly slicked down. I was convinced that somewhere on his attire he would sport his initials. Sure enough, they were on his tie clip, and prominent on the handkerchief in his breast pocket. His smile was purposeful and cheery, his voice high and persuasive. I was resigned to walk into the trap, my mind too tired to resist. What do I care what makes him tick? I thought. I know what kind of machine I want. I'll get it over with as quickly as possible. But why today, of all days? Despite the artificial brightness of the store, I felt the dark despair of the remembered night clutching at me. I should be walking alone somewhere, thinking of Ilse and how desperately she had struggled to go on living. I wasn't prepared for the salesman's opening gambit. He said something with great emphasis, probably a repetition of what he had asked.

"Well, Honey, is there anything I can help you with? What do you have in mind?"

"An automatic," I answered dully, my voice sounding strange and stupid.

"We don't sell any manual machines."

Now I could almost hear him repeat the conversation to his wife that evening, "Oh, boy, did I have a kooky dame tonight . . .," then slump down in front of his TV, a can of beer in his hand. I'm really not being fair to him, I thought. He can't know, after all.

"Look," I said, getting back to reality with some effort. "I'm interested in the simplest machine you have, preferably one with a large tub."

"Oh, I can show you that." He waved his hand in a deprecating gesture. "But first let me show you something very special."

I obediently trotted behind him and came to a platform covered with silver foil. It was ablaze with a tangle of colored lights. A large machine, obviously one of the latest technical wonders, stood in the center. There was an array of pastel buttons and gleaming knobs, quite modernistic looking, I had to admit to myself.

"Now here you have our new 'Lady Domore,' and that's no joke. Like having a maid in the house." Pride was creeping into his voice. "Automatically puts in bleach and bluing. On sale today, too. Just three hundred fifty-nine dollars. Ten dollars down. Your neighbor's eyes will pop out with envy when she sees this one. And that's this week only. April twenty-ninth to the sixth of May—jubilee week—you're in luck."

Yes, I realized.

"The twenty-ninth must be kind of a special day, is it?"

"It's special all right, a good day to get this Lady Domore," he wound up with emphasis.

"Or a fine day to die." It was just barely audible.

He looked at me guardedly, not knowing whether he had heard correctly, but without pressing the point further. I could see it confirmed, though, that he thought his initial impression had been right. He was clearly dealing with some sort of nut, but his training wouldn't let him ease up. "Tell you what. I can write it up for you. You'll be glad you came in today. Can't beat a Lady Domore."

"No, I guess not," I mumbled, my mind screaming that they beat Ilse on the day she died.

"I really had been thinking of something simpler," I forced myself to offer in a more normal tone of voice. "Those buttons would get me all confused."

"Oh, come on now, you look bright. Bet you could persuade your husband to get you anything you want. You'd learn them buttons fast. See the pink one here? That's for lukewarm water, and red is for hot, blue for cold."

"Blue for cold," I repeated mechanically. The water I got from the brook for Ilse was cold, too. It felt icy when it trickled from my fingers to Ilse's parched lips, and they were hot.

"Yes, I get it," I said, and he broke into a smile.

"You're catching on fast. Not hard to learn, now, is it?"

I turned away, unable to face the monstrous machine, and out of the corner of my eye saw him shrug his shoulders. But he patiently walked me to the far corner of the store, to which the poor relations of the Lady Domore had been relegated.

"You wouldn't want that one, now, would you?" He was pointing toward a machine that showed only three buttons. He looked at me shrewdly, allowing sufficient time to elapse for the comparison to sink in.

"Why? What's wrong with it?"

My question seemed to take him by surprise. His manner implied that any person with eyes must be able to see the difference. The tone of his voice dropped lower, a note of regret creeping into it. "Motor's the same, but no automatic water regulator. You'll have to regulate the faucet."

"You mean by hand?" I tried to sound incredulous. "You mean I have to get the water from the faucet?" I had to stop myself from saying "from the brook." But my irony was lost on him, although he quickly recovered.

"Good sense of humor you have, Honey." He made one last attempt. "Why don't you send your husband in? Bet he'll get you the Lady Domore. *He'll* understand the difference."

His well-trained eyes were scanning the aisles, coming to rest on the next one over. A resolute-looking young couple was giving the Lady Domore the once-over; then they were promptly intercepted by another salesman. For a moment his face fell. I was beginning to feel guilty. I really wasn't being fair to him. After all, it was his livelihood to sell washing machines—certainly not to know and assess my past. And if he did know, would he understand?

In a more civil tone, I heard myself saying, "Would you mind explaining the water levels again, please?" And that made him fall into his routine, rapidly and competently rattling off the information.

"And what's that for?" I asked, pointing to a knob he hadn't explained before.

"That's the speed control. You have two speeds: regular and delicate."

"Pretty clever. A machine for delicate people."

Now he didn't know whether to laugh or give up on me.

"How much is it?"

"Normally, two forty-nine, but because of jubilee week, it's only two nineteen, plus tax."

"I'll take it," I said quickly, handing him my charge plate. "When can I get it delivered?"

For a moment he was taken aback. "Oh, you have to understand, I have nothing to do with delivery." His words came out in spurts, and he appeared to be wrestling with the question of whether he had done everything possible. "You'll have it within a week, for sure."

Within a week! What was racing through my mind was the promise I had made to Ilse to hang on for another week, a time during which my life hung in the balance. Now the prize at the end of this coming week would be a gleaming white washing machine with two speeds, three water levels, and two rinse cycles (one deep rinse and a separate one for delicate fabrics).

Lost in thought, I drove home, took off my wet raincoat, gave the girls a bath, doused their itching skin with calamine lotion, put on their pajamas, and tucked them into bed. The baby woke up, so I changed him and gave him a bottle, after which he fell asleep in my arms. Putting him in his crib, I mechanically turned on the night-light. Kurt came up to kiss the girls goodnight; then we both went down to the kitchen for a cup of tea and some brownies I had baked that afternoon. To complete the routine, we went to the den, picked up the evening paper, and settled in.

So many memories of April 29, stretching over more than half a century. Bright days, dull days, good days, and bad days, infused with the pain of knowing what had been given to me, while Ilse was deprived of everything. Milestones marking the road of my life.

It snowed heavily on April 29, 1999. The traffic in Boston was reduced to a crawl as Kurt and I were approaching a site along the Freedom Trail. With us was a group of approximately forty people, part of another generation, but seemingly from another world. They were members of YPO, Young Presidents Organization, the prestigious group of movers and shakers of the corporate world. They were laboring to make their way over the snowbanks that led to Boston's Holocaust Memorial.

There stood six tall columns, in stark outline against the darkened sky, like giant accusing fingers. Etched into the transparent panes that form the sides of the towers are a multitude of numbers—millions of them—commemorating those deprived of their identity, known to their oppressors merely as numbers. On each side of the memorial thoughts are engraved, quotes from Holocaust survivors' writings. One column bears a quote by Primo Levi. Another, from my autobiography, reads: "Ilse, a childhood friend of mine, once found a raspberry. She carried it in her pocket all day to present it to me that night on a leaf she had plucked through the barbed wire. Imagine a world in which your entire possession is one crushed raspberry and you give it to your friend." Ilse, her name and deed etched into stone, on a memorial located on America's beloved trail of freedom in the city of Boston.

I HAVE VISITED THAT SITE MANY TIMES IN MANY SEASONS: in bright sunlight and during the lonely hours of the night. I have watched people stop and read the inscriptions. The young, the old—what are their thoughts? During one of my visits, I saw a young man read it, walk away, then turn and come back to read it again. What was coursing through his mind and what image did he retain of Ilse?

Although there is no marker on her lonely grave, her name and her sacrifice are etched for all time to come on this cherished ground of American history. It comforts me to know that no monuments have been erected to Hitler and his venom, but there *are* monuments to freedom and to the nobility of spirit, such as Ilse possessed.

In 2001, when that significant date rolled around, I filled the day with a variety of simple chores, aside from the errands described, while thoughts and memories of my friend flashed intermittently through my mind. However, at the end of the day, when I went to bed, sleep would not come. Slowly, without waking Kurt, I crept out of bed, noting from the clock that it was seven minutes to midnight. My steps took me to the flower-laden patio, into the soft Arizona night. It was very quiet, and the air was motionless. The moon was silvery golden, and the stars stretched to infinity. Ilse's face, serene, tender, and young, floated from the recesses of my mind. Ilse, you were younger then than my granddaughters are now. Oh, Ilse, will we ever understand what happened?

Another April 29 was fading into the night, to give way to another day. And tomorrow—yes, tomorrow—I will have to mail the letters I forgot to send today; they are tucked in the visor over the windshield of my car. And yes, I forgot to return the books to the library and will have to pay a late fee on some of them. Ilse, barely conscious, you whispered, "Why?"

Why then, I repeat, am I here and you are not?

Ilse, as a young child,
with her father in Bielsko, Poland

Château on the Marne, Part I

*T*HE NEW YEAR OPENED WITH GREAT PROMISE. The sound of "1950" had a nice ring to it. It was the start of the second half of the twentieth century. The first had seen so much misery and war; this promised to hold peace and real happiness. I, for one, was blissfully happy. We had just moved from our small apartment into a spacious one with three large bedrooms that afforded our eighteen-month-old Vivie a sunny nursery with a large bay window. It was there that I had put her down for her afternoon nap, going downstairs to collect the mail.

One envelope leaped out immediately, because of its familiar red-and-blue border, filling me with happy anticipation. As I expected, it was a letter from my uncle, who had recently moved from Istanbul to Paris. Whenever they came, his communications were like harbingers of fascinating and exciting news. It seemed that wherever he resided, he would imaginatively indulge in his philatelic obsession. Never in all the years we had written to each other did I receive a letter bearing merely a single stamp. A large part of each envelope was always taken up by a magnitude of stamps, showing portraits of prominent personages, reproductions of historical buildings, or flora and fauna in all shapes and colors. To top it off, my uncle never trusted the postal system when it came to delivery. Thus a letter addressed to me from Paris would bear the inscriptions *Madame* and *Mrs.*, followed by my name and address in large printed letters. That was rounded out by USA, ÉTATS-UNIS, AMERICA.

41

After which he added a sticker proclaiming PAR AVION and hand-printed BY AIRMAIL. For good measure, in case some postal employees could read neither French nor English, he would also add the German word LUFTPOST. The entire legend was underlined with red and blue pencil.

My mother, in her copious letters to her brother in Turkey, had carried such things to greater extremes. I remember that she not only heavily underlined ISTANBUL but also added CONSTANTINOPLE. (I am fairly certain, but not positive, that she did not also add BYZANTIUM for good measure.) I must confess that I too have been touched by that type of idiosyncrasy. Because my handwriting is almost illegible, I do make sure that envelops bear much hand-printed detail.

Mama and her brother were born during the reign of Emperor Franz Joseph of Austria, in a small but generally thriving town called Bielitz, to which the townspeople proudly and affectionately referred to as *Klein-Wien*—mini-Vienna. (No record exists, on the other hand, that the citizens of Vienna referred to their city as *Gross-Bielitz*—maxi-Bielitz). The prosperity of Bielitz can be traced to the excellence of its weaving factories, which produced the finest woolen fabrics in Poland, despite the fact that Lodz was a larger city by far and boasted many more mills. The burghers of Bielitz looked down on those of Lodz, insisting that the latter's fabrics were of inferior quality, meant for the masses. Bielitz's textiles, on the other hand, were literally "fit for kings." The finest wool, the most discreet and conservative patterns, woven into fabrics of a quality for which the town was renowned. And that carried over into the attitude Bielitz's residents adopted for themselves. They quite confidently considered themselves superior in every respect, particularly when it came to culture.

That was the milieu that shaped my mother and my uncle, imbuing them with those attitudes. My mother was the older, born in 1898, followed by her brother in 1900. No more glaring differences could have existed between two siblings than were revealed in their personalities. Aside from their individual character traits, my mother still seemed to belong to the century in which she was born. Her behavior and attitude reflected the mores of the Victorian era, whereas my uncle, from early childhood, was clearly a son of the new century. He firmly believed in its unlimited possibilities, and his daring and energy burst from every pore of his being to explore them fully. He was to own one of the first motor-cycles in town, which he drove with great speed if not recklessness. On the other hand, my mother's favorite entertainment, once the morning chores were done, was to change her blouse or dress, comb her hair, and then spray some of her favorite eau de cologne, such 4711 or Tosca, around her neck. She would proceed to pour herself a cup of coffee, using one of the better porcelain cups, and then seat herself near the window where the light was best for working on her needlepoint.

Although my mother was by outspoken consensus a real beauty, com-pliments never seemed to go to her head. She was somewhat reticent, quiet, and unassuming. Feature for feature, sister and brother resembled each other to an astounding degree. They had the same blue-black wavy hair and huge, velvety, deep brown eyes. Whereas Leopold's were charged with a restless electricity, hers were unfathomable pools of serenity. He was constantly in motion, to the point of appearing driven, while she seemed eternally in repose. There could not have been two people so much alike on the surface, yet so totally different in reality. He adored her, and she worshipped him.

Though I would overhear a good deal of family lore from the adults around me, it always came with the admonition not to repeat it to "out-siders." After giving birth to my brother, my mother was considered of "delicate health." On the advice of her doctor, she decided to take "the cure" in a nearby Czech spa, quite likely Karlsbad. Frugal as she was, Mother checked into a modest *pension*, taking mud baths and drinking allegedly strength-giving *Sprudel*, the local sparkling mineral water. In the course of her stay, she befriended other young women, two of whom were single. Exchanging the usual gossip, she found that they were madly, hopelessly in love with a mysterious young nobleman who, needless to say, was oblivious to their feelings. They knew his habit of emerging from the best hotel in town at the stroke of noon, usually for a short stroll or a *Fiaker* ride, often leaving a host of adoring looks and a chorus of sighs in his wake. (This was still the time of the barely bygone roman-tic era that had seen Crown Prince Rudolf's suicide with his young mis-tress, Maria Vetsera, whose perpetually flower-strewn grave was to become the site of pilgrimage for countless unhappy lovers.)

Mother, curious to see this paragon of masculine virtues, accompanied her two friends to the Hotel Imperial shortly before noon. Punctuality being the courtesy of kings and noblemen, the imposing portal at the top of the stone steps opened at the stroke of noon, and a figure, dressed impeccably in white, with matching white fedora hat and carrying a black, silver-topped cane, emerged. Tall, dashing, debonair, the man descended the steps with élan, stopped halfway down, and, like a general surveying a battlefield, looked around him before making his way to the street. Once he got close to where Mother stood, he removed his fedora in a sweeping gesture, bowed deeply, kissed her hand, and then retreated toward a horse-drawn carriage waiting in front of the hotel. Mother stood transfixed, rooted to the spot. Her companions were incredulous: "Do you know him? Do you know the baron?" And to the young ladies' consternation, she informed them that the "baron" was her brother.

Under certain circumstances, my uncle's noble bearing could extend even further. His first name, Leopold, had a distinguished ring to it and was not uncommon in the circles of Austrian and German nobility. Knowing as well that his last name sounded distinguished, he at times—and "only for fun, mind you" —inserted a small *von* between his first and last names. His parents were not amused. Adding to his cachet of nobility and higher education was a long, narrow scar on his cheek, hardly discernible but similar to those found on the faces of students at the renowned University of Heidelberg, as evidence of their membership in one of its dueling fraternities—a relationship he had a deft way of neither confirming nor denying.

A few evenings later, under the cover of darkness and using the servants' entrance, Leopold made his way to Mama's modest *pension*. Actually the visit was not motivated strictly by fraternal love; rather it was to petition Mother to grant him a small loan that would see him through his next "baronial" expenses. It must be added, though, that he would unfailingly repay those debts, usually accompanied by a gift that often exceeded the amount of the loan. It was equally true that, had he *never* repaid those sums, Mother would still have considered it her privilege to indulge him.

HE ALWAYS LIVED ON A LARGE SCALE, and for the most of his life, he managed to travel first class, literally and figuratively. Papa told us one story that in particular bears this out. He became the unwitting observer of his brother-in-law's verve at a point when Uncle Leopold's fortunes had hit a nadir. He was casting about for a position or association that would rescue him from his financial dilemma.

It so happened that my father had traveled to another city, where he heard about an opening in a firm that sounded suitable for his brother-in-law. He wasted no time sending Leopold a telegram, in which he suggested a meeting between the potential employer and my uncle, something Leopold accepted with alacrity.

In due time, accompanied by my father, the man went to the station to meet my uncle. The train pulled in, passengers got off, but there was no sign of Leopold. Finally, when the platform was nearly empty, the door of a first-class compartment swung open and, allowing for a dramatic entrance, Leopold emerged from its red plush interior, impeccably dressed as usual.

Questioned later about his extravagance, he let on to my father that he had traveled third class all the way to the previous station, from where, after having paid the conductor, he was able to complete the last stretch in style.

My father was not impressed, nor was the would-be employer, who confided to my father that his operation was far too small to offer a place for someone of his brother-in-law's taste and talents. That soon held true for Leopold's environment as well. Bielitz/Bielsko was too narrow, too small a canvas, for the panorama of Leopold's life. My hometown had been ceded to Poland after World War I, becoming Bielsko. Leopold did not speak Polish, nor did he relish the prospect of learning it, his training as a textile engineer having been in German. Differences of opinion had always existed between him and his father, and after one particular quarrel, he decided to leave home. He would go as far away as possible. Family legend had it that one evening he spread the map of Europe on the dining room table, announcing grandiloquently that he would blindfold himself and wherever his finger would point, that was where he would go to seek his fortune. My grandfather left the room, Grandmother kept a stiff upper lip, and Mother broke into tears, but at the end of this little charade, he dramatically made clear that Turkey would be his destination. Those who knew him well were convinced that the blindfold was not totally tight, and that he had kept his eye all along on what he called *das Land der unbegrenzten Möglichkeiten*—the country of unlimited possibilities. Kemal Atatürk was modernizing Turkey, abolishing harems, and making sweeping changes in the old customs. He would need young, energetic, and imaginative people to build up the country's economy. What better than to offer his services as a textile engineer was Leopold's rationale. For him the lure of the remote, the exotic, the unexplored was irresistible.

While his father predicted that he would be back in no time, with apologies for his follies, his stern mother warned about many unknown dangers that awaited him in such a strange environment. But Leopold remained adamant. Before leaving, he entrusted to my father the filial duties he himself would be unable to carry out. And in most ways, Papa succeeded admirably in doing just that over the ensuring years. My brother lost his best playmate, though. (I remember none of it, having been too young.) When it came time for Leopold to leave, my mother was inconsolable. No sooner had her brother departed than she brought forth a large piece of stationery and in her steady, beautiful script began to write him a letter, the first of countless such missives she would send off on an almost daily basis. From then on his presence was always with her, as hers must have been with him, for rare was the week that did not bring at least two or three messages from him. That held true until the war started.

The dire predictions of Leopold's parent did not materialize. Instead, he prospered and succeeded far beyond anybody's expectations except his own. He would visit us twice a year, usually combining them with business trips that would further his burgeoning textile production. To me, during the early years of my childhood, he was a figure from some enchanted kingdom, a sultan, a pasha, arriving on a magic carpet, his bags bulging with exotic gifts. Once, when I was about nine or ten years old, he asked what wishes I might have, and I indicated that there was nothing I wanted more than an Angora cat. So he traveled to Vienna on the Orient Express and from there to Bielsko. He arrived, cage in hand, holding the much-desired cat, a blue silk ribbon around its neck. My grandmother was scandalized, for the cat's diet was to include fish, something that she reserved solely for gefilte fish, a staple for the Sabbath meal. Each time he came, there would be small barrels of halvah, Turkish honey with green pistachios, but also exotic earrings, harem bracelets, and yards of heavy black silk for Grandmother's dresses. A meerschaum pipe might be a typical gift for Papa, but the nicest, most expensive gifts were always meant for his beloved sister.

As it turned out, he tried to get us to leave Poland when war became imminent. In a dramatic cable, he announced that visas were waiting for us at the embassy in Warsaw and urged us to leave without delay. However, two weeks earlier, Papa had suffered a heart attack, so Mama simply put the dispatch into her apron pocket, saying, "We can't upset Papa at a time like this." With that the Weissmann family's fate was sealed. I only hope and pray she never realized what she had brought about by trying to protect Papa's health.

After the outbreak of the war, Uncle Leopold continued his valiant efforts to help us, sending packages whenever it was possible. Later, after the war, finding me, the only surviving member of our family, he focused his attention on me with unrestrained generosity, caring, and gifts. There was no end to his concern about me. His inquiries about my health during my pregnancy were touching, and he responded exuberantly when he heard that I had delivered a child without complications. He did, however, find it necessary to apologize to Kurt on my behalf because it was a girl. When photos of her showed an unmistakable resemblance to my mother, his joy was unrestrained.

What I had not realized in the early joyful communications with my uncle was the fact that at that time his marriage had turned into a disaster. A bitter divorce followed, after which he decided to leave Turkey and move to Paris, and as far as I knew, that had given him a certain peace of mind.

Full of happy anticipation, I sat down then to savor the contents of this latest communication. The first paragraphs, which dealt with the baby, were rather more lengthy than usual, as if he were hesitating to convey some news. He had been to Switzerland on business, and, while there, decided to consult a specialist about a persistent hoarseness that had been bothering him for while. It had not diminished over a period of time, and the doctors in Turkey and France attributed it to his heavy smoking. That was hardly a surprise, his habit being to smoke two to three packs a day. Then came the bombshell: The Zurich specialist's diagnosis was POSITIVE.

The word leaped out at me, printed in large capitals as it was. It was as if he had wanted to break the pen as he was writing it. At first I didn't understand, or perhaps didn't want to. Lamely I read on; he had undergone surgery for cancer in Zurich and was having radiation treatments at the American Hospital in Paris. Here he drew a line across the letter that ran from edge to edge, as if he wanted to separate what he had written from what was to come. Below the line was a new salutation to Kurt and me, but he addressed it mostly to Kurt, asking permission for me to travel to Paris. He wanted to see me as soon as possible. I broke into sobs, not reading the rest of the letter. Instead I ran to the phone to notify Kurt. I had not seen my uncle since the summer of 1937, when I was thirteen.

We sent him a cable late that night, informing him that I would come to Paris as soon as it could be arranged. For a number of weeks, dispatches crossed between Buffalo and Paris amid a flurry of hasty preparations. No travel arrangements to Europe were routine at that time, and obtaining a passport, a visa, and booking a seat on a flight presented formidable obstacles. We were able to solve another problem, however. Kurt's sister in New York City would take the baby.

The news of my impending trip and the sad reason that occasioned it spread through my circle of friends, but their concern was mixed with the excitement that such an adventure generated at that time. Even though I was aware of the fact that in all likelihood I would be spending most of the time in the hospital or at his sickbed at home, I nevertheless felt I needed to look presentable for Paris. After all, I wouldn't want to embarrass my uncle in front of his friends and business acquaintances by my lack of finesse when it came to couture. I knew that he moved in some rather distinguished circles, and so I enlisted a few of my friends' help in preparing my modest wardrobe. A trip to Paris by air was still sufficiently uncommon to have the local paper, the *Buffalo Evening News*, arrange with Air France for a publicity photo of me standing on the steps that led to the plane's door, about to board, wearing a fetching cloche with veil and clutching in my gloved hand a smart purse that had come as part of the deal with the hat. (They came from a modest hat shop and had set me back all of twelve dollars.)

With heavy heart, I kissed my husband and child good-bye and headed back to Europe, to which I had vowed earlier never to return. It was a long night flight, one weighted with many thoughts: gratitude for what America had given me—my husband and baby; a home, secure and filled with love; a true haven. In the course of the four years I had lived there, it had healed many wounds. I was fearful of Europe, fearful of what I would find, and braced myself to confront a presumably old, very ill man. During my formative years, I had considered him more glamorous than any movie star. Would I recognize him, would he be well enough to meet me at the airport?

The plane touched down on the runway of Le Bourget, the ground wet from the night's rain. There followed the usual arrival formalities, making it difficult for me to contain my anxiety and impatience. Once I had gone through customs, there stood Uncle Leopold, still an imposing figure of a man, and we flew into each other's arms. I detected a faint and delicious scent that stirred some indefinable memories. We held each other in a long, wordless embrace. Then he pushed me away at arm's length to give me a once-over. I could only look at him, tears streaming down both our faces. "You don't look like your mother," he whispered, wiping his eyes with a handkerchief, "but her blood flows in your veins." With that he embraced me again.

To my surprise and delight, he did not look ill at all. He was deeply tanned and exuded elegance and sophistication. He was accompanied by a male secretary who immediately busied himself with my luggage. Marcel, the chauffeur, greeted me with a stiff bow and a formal "Madame." As in a dream, we drove through the glistening early-morning streets of Paris to the Place Vendôme, where my uncle kept a suite at the Hotel Calais as his pied-à-terre. He let on that there was someone who was "most eager" to meet me. Although tired from the long flight, I agreed without a moment's hesitation to meet his friend.

When she arrived, she immediately intimidated me. Very chic, in a black *tailleur*, she wore a scarf that fell down onto the jacket of her smart suit. A heavy gold necklace, from which hung an enormous cross with large amethysts, completed her aura of French haute couture. I wondered briefly whether she had some association with a religious order, but as soon as she opened her jacket, I saw the extent of the décolletage, and it came back to me that amethysts were my uncle's favorite gems. She approached me, obviously scrutinizing every detail of my appearance, and I subsequently wondered whether she had decided from the start that she had nothing to fear. Or did she? We were never to get closer to each other, and always kept a polite distance during my entire stay.

Initially I was greatly relieved that my uncle appeared not to be as ill as his dramatic summons had indicated, and harbored high hopes for his eventual recovery. This belief was reinforced by the fact that he was deeply involved in the renovation and decoration of a large villa—actually more a small château—he had recently purchased, situated on the Marne. This was all more surprising in view of the plans he had revealed in his letters. It was his intention to emigrate to Canada as soon as possible. He wanted to be near us, he had emphasized, and I was apprehensive that his illness might forestall such a move. Although somewhat reassured by this unexpected turn, I was still greatly puzzled by his decision to acquire the French property. Timid as I was, I refrained from asking too many questions, perhaps sustaining my childhood faith in such "adult" decisions being wise and correct. It was a matter of special pride to him, he let on, to call the estate Trois Lions, in honor of his three young sons, whom he had placed in various boarding schools in France and Switzerland.

I couldn't help but reflect that I was now twice the age I had been when I had last seen my uncle. I was approaching my twenty-sixth birthday, whereas my uncle was fifty. Seeing him after such a long interval, I regarded him with different eyes. Women eyed me with envy wherever we went, and he was not averse to the signals they sent. He had always had an eye for beautiful women, nodding and bowing to them in restaurants in his most charming manner. There would be times, I was to find out, when he would ask the waiter to take a bottle of champagne, with his compliments, to the object of his attention. I pretended to be oblivious to those charades, although in reality I felt scandalized by them. But I could clearly see the effect he had on women. He had a commanding presence, coupled with an animal magnetism. His dress without question was Saville Row, something to which he imparted his own distinctive look. It was with special dash that he wore his cream-colored silk, monogrammed, custom-made shirts, and he told me one of his secrets: He would have the collar cut in a way that emphasized his permanently tanned neck, and his cuffs were made longer, so as to permit his exotic cufflinks to show. He wore a gold link bracelet in an age when that was considered a feminine ornament; yet, on his wrist, it became the epitome of masculinity. He told me how he once created a sensation at a ball when he appeared in a midnight blue tuxedo. He owned forty suits but considered it vulgar to have more, as he allowed with a wicked smile. He stressed that he always gave one away when acquiring a new one.

While dining in restaurants, we would talk a great deal, and the subject would often turn to my mother. Whenever he spoke of her, he would stop eating, put his knife and fork down, and put his hand on mine, as if trying to touch her through me. I would catch some beautiful, elegant woman who had been eyeing him, observing that affectionate gesture, sizing me up, puzzled at what she found, wondering where I fitted in this scheme of things. I wanted to be able to shout: *Relax, I'm his niece!* But whenever *I* brought up a subject even remotely related to my mother during the war years, he instantly switched the conversation to another topic. There were times when he would brusquely cut me off. Naturally I was hurt, for she was *my* mother, after all. I, too, yearned to share my thoughts, my admiration of her, the pain of my own loss, of being orphaned so young.

The truth was that I was still in need of a mother and a father. Subconsciously, I suppose, I was looking for a father figure in him, for some tangible trait that my own beloved father had possessed, and that I could identify in my uncle. I wanted to be praised by my uncle for having coped as a teenager, for having played a role in supporting my parents mentally and physically during those difficult years in the dark cellar of our home and, later, in the miserable Jewish ghetto in Bielsko. I had to admit that, sitting in those elegant Paris restaurants, it seemed incongruous to talk about such matters, but I had an overriding need to give vent to them. I wanted him to understand how painful it was for me that my parents never knew my beloved husband, never saw their beautiful grandchild. But he would not listen. He merely would stress how much Mama would enjoy the château, how she would like and appreciate his precious Gobelins and vases. I would respond in a perfunctory way, never going further than to nod assent. I might come back, "Yes, especially after she had to give up—" but he would abruptly cut me off and bow to a woman at an adjacent table.

I was too young, too inexperienced, to understand his side of it. I could not grasp his pain, his guilt, and his regret. He must have reasoned that, after all, I had been there with my parents to share that misery with them: the cold, the hunger, the despair. During all that time, he had lived in luxury, growing ever more affluent, while his beloved sister . . . I didn't need to finish his thought processes when it came to me years later what he must have felt and how I had lacked the experience to understand him. My youth had take such an abnormal turn when I was fifteen that, on the one hand, I was mature far beyond my actual age after the war; while on the other, any conventional development had stopped and atrophied at that point of my adolescence. When we met again after those traumatic experiences, I did not understand that he needed to get away from his guilt, self-imposed as it was. His love for my mother, his guilt over not sharing her fate, drove him to those endless explorations of antique shops, to hunt for yet more bibelots—the trinkets, the wall sconces, the furnishings he was amassing for his new home. His pride at being able to find and afford to buy a bed that was reputed to have belonged to Napoleon—its bedposts boasting the requisite eagles, richly carved and gilded—showed clearly. Was the bed authentic? I truly don't know. Yet I understand now what I did not have the maturity to realize then: how much he wanted to be able to show all that to his sister, and how painful it was for him that I was not an image of her. And yet he would go on trying to find her in me.

On one of those occasions, a balmy evening in early May, we decided to walk from a restaurant where we had enjoyed a fine dinner to Leopold's pied-à-terre, for we were staying in town overnight. It would be best, because he had an early appointment at the American Hospital. On the way, he asked a question relating to his children. We came to a halt in front of a well-known jeweler's window glittering with an array of exquisite gems. The most precious ones had apparently been locked up for the night, but a few of the lesser ones were still alluringly displayed. Not wanting to answer his question, I resorted to one of his tricks by changing the subject. Feigning a sudden interest in a beautiful bracelet, I drew his attention to it. He put his arm around me, pulled me closer, and said: "Tell me I'm right, and I'll buy you that bracelet." I could not agree with him; as a matter of fact, I thought he was dead wrong, so I refrained from answering. He persisted until I finally just shook my head. I saw his lip twitch, a hard line etched around his chin. He let go of my arm and started to walk away. Silently, I walked behind him, then caught up, tears stinging my eyelids. I would have loved to have that bracelet, but I couldn't do it.

For years that moment came back to haunt me at the most unexpected times. I remembered the pain I had caused him, perhaps unnecessarily. With shame, I thought of my mother; she would have told him a hundred times that he was right and would actually have believed it. Could I not have agreed with him even if I actually disagreed, just to make him feel good? Why was I so judgmental, so sanctimonious and priggish? How could I have been so narrow-minded, so selfish, as to cause a mortally ill man, whom I professed to love, so much pain? Over the years, I would wake up some nights in anguish, thinking of my uncharitable attitude. And each time the incident came back, the pain and regret had not diminished. A few decades later, something happened that was a revelation to me. In the process of cleaning out a drawer, while throwing away a bottle of hardened nail polish, an awareness hit me like a thunderbolt: Yes, I had done right. Oh, God, what happened in front of that jewelry store had been the right thing to do. He was upset, felt hurt and humiliated. But later, much later, he must have realized the truth. I prayed that he had come to that realization, and that it was a comfort to him. He was used to hearing what he wanted to hear, to see others in agreement with him. He was used to paying for flattery, to buying opinions. No question, I hurt him, I caused him pain, but I knew that it must have shown him how much I loved him for himself. I felt elated—grateful, even—that I had given him tangible proof of my love. Had I gotten that bracelet, it would have been tainted with shame.

The Château on the Marne

Château on the Marne, Part II

DURING MY STAY WITH UNCLE LEOPOLD, whenever I mentioned my departure from Paris, he would get upset, at times showing his anger. I felt there was something undefined, unfinished between us. It was no easy task to delve into these matters, but whenever I mustered enough courage to do so, he diverted the question. I was particularly eager to discuss his planned move to Canada. We had found out that, contrary to the stringent requirements imposed by the U.S. immigration system, Canada was more liberal and actually welcomed people with money. There were, however, a few problems to be solved. To begin with, he was stateless, never having obtained Polish citizenship after our part of Austria became Poland following World War I. Although married to a Turkish citizen, he never succeeded in obtaining citizenship of that country either. Given his statelessness, I assume that his business interests in France enabled him to establish French residency. But also due to his statelessness, any travel that he contemplated was extremely complicated. Often he would ask me to show him my passport. He would hold it with awe, exclaiming, "What I wouldn't give to have this!" And I was proud and grateful to be an American, to belong at last to a place that wanted me.

When I suggested that we should move faster in regard to his Canada project, he would insist that I had become too American. Americans had no patience, and their motto was Hurry, hurry. I would be angry, yet pleased as well, for I desperately wanted to be as American as possible.

Even then I dimly perceived the underlying reason for his procrastination. He was stalling for time, sensing that perhaps there was not too much of it left. He once told me a story I no longer remember in its entirety, but it dealt with someone deceiving the Grim Reaper by not taking a certain route he had indicated he would take. But, of course, death caught up with him on his alternate route.

Leopold was extremely superstitious, as was my mother. Although he believed in kismet, or fate, he nevertheless felt that one could perhaps circumvent it. Was that why he kept talking about Canada while getting the French château ready for a prolonged stay? I felt the unresolved knot in our relationship was still based on his hope that I would somehow assume my mother's personality. What I didn't realize then was that he had recently lost his anchor. His marriage, no matter how bad, had provided some stability. He had had to give up most of what he had built up over the years, and any new venture would be fraught with a great deal of uncertainty in a new and strange business climate. That is why, in all likelihood, he pinned his hopes on me to restore some normality, an expectation to which he clung tenaciously. I, on the other hand, despite the enormity of what I had lost during the war, had now gained a husband, a child, a home, and a country. By any measure, those were the things he craved. Having spent more than a month with my uncle, I wanted nothing so much as to go home, assuaging my pangs of conscience by rationalizing that once he and his children got to Canada, we would be able to make up for lost time. Regrettably, I did not understand the full implications of his present state of affairs, instead coping clumsily and erratically with the situation.

It came as a relief, therefore, when he informed me that before my departure for the States, he wanted me to do an important thing for him—hand-deliver some papers to his banker in Switzerland. My stay in Zurich would be brief, and there would be a bonus: I would be able to visit Kurt's elderly relatives, who had shown great kindness to the entire family during the war. I loved the idea of going to Switzerland; everything about it would be fascinating and beautiful. Paris made me feel inferior, because the French can easily give you that complex. My French is poor and not grammatical; I always had to be on my toes to strain and understand what was being said. The imposing majesty of Paris made me feel insignificant, much like a country bumpkin among those ultrachic Parisiennes. Switzerland would be a different story. First of all, they spoke German, the language with which I had grown up. I would be able to get around without any problems, and I expected that Swiss women would not be as intimidating.

Once in Zurich, I found it effortless to take care of my uncle's business matter, in total contrast to what I had encountered when dealing with French officialdom. It felt wonderful to be welcomed with open arms by Aunt Katinka and her kindly husband, who reminded me of my grandparents. This was the closest thing to walking back into my childhood, and a state of nostalgia and well-being enveloped me. The massive old-fashioned furniture and appointments seemed like a bastion of safety reminiscent of earlier days. It was soothing to engage in warm, caring conversation, and we spoke of my hosts' relatives in Buffalo, who had become mine as well. To top it off, they endlessly admired photos of my baby. It all came as a welcome antidote to the formality and stiffness of my uncle's two domains in and outside Paris. Later, in my room, it was sheer bliss to thrust open the tall windows, letting in the scent of lilacs from the garden, then to crawl under the feather-light eiderdown quilts and go to sleep.

I awoke to a cloudless May morning that was my twenty-sixth birthday, much like the birthdays I remembered from home. Should I tell my hosts about it? But no, that wouldn't do. They would fret, try to do something special, buy me gifts. But the old feeling of anticipation, the idea of the singularity of the day that was bred into me, began to stir. I wanted so much to tell someone, to have someone acknowledge its meaning to me. It occurred to me that I could cut my stay short, return to Paris, despite the warmth that engulfed me here. After all, Kurt might try to call me there, and I would surely have mail from him that contained longed-for news, or even photos of the baby. My longing intensified. At breakfast I revealed my decision to go back to Paris and, despite my hosts' insistence that I stay longer, was able to make my point, using concern about my uncle's health as an excuse. With their help, I dispatched a cable to Uncle Leopold's office, apprising him of my arrival in Paris that evening.

My uncle's secretary had secured my ticket, and, of course, it was first class. To travel even third class on Swiss trains is a luxury, whereas first class exceeds all expectations. Deep leather club chairs, huge windows, and every conceivable comfort were at my disposal. I felt somewhat ill at ease, as if intruding in a place where I did not belong. Before the train departed, a beautiful blond woman, wearing a cream-colored silk blouse, entered the compartment, tossed an enormous alligator bag to the floor, rummaged in it, and from its flame-red interior extracted some papers. Scooping up the bag, she unaccountably left, trailing the fragrance of an exotic perfume. The brief encounter left me all the more aware of the contrast between her appearance and mine. Suddenly my pride and joy, a spanking white Ship 'n' Shore blouse, felt cheap, if not vulgar. Who was she? Certainly upper crust. In any event, she was at home in this milieu, and I was not. Fortunately she did not return.

At the last minute, just before the train was off to an almost imperceptible start, a man entered and took the seat across from mine. While he was getting settled, my attention was diverted by the now rapidly changing landscape, having left the station now behind us, and before long a spectacular panorama began to unfold outside the window. Feeling better in anticipation of getting back to Paris and receiving mail, and thinking of my birthday, I scrutinized the man across from me: elderly by my count, no doubt in his fifties. His appearance gave the impression of understated expensive attire, and to my surprise he was reading the London *Times*. Before I could restrain myself, I blurted out, "Oh, you read English!" He lowered the paper and, in a mixture of irritation and amusement, came back in a clipped English accent, "It might surprise you, but some people do."

Embarrassed, I tried to explain. "You see, I haven't spoken English in more than five weeks, and I do miss it." That seemed to satisfy him, especially in view of my accent. No one would have been surprised if I had spoken no English at all. Exchanging a few pleasantries led to the inevitable question of where I was from, and to a smile when I mentioned Buffalo. His next question made me blush. Was Buffalo a city renowned for its pretty girls? Again to my embarrassment, I blurted out that I had never noticed. Fortunately, he immersed himself in the *Times* again, giving me a chance to concentrate on the landscape. After a while, I became aware that he was eyeing me again. It was a quizzical look, no doubt due to his puzzlement as to what I was doing in first class. I could feel him scrutinizing me, taking in the well-manicured nails Uncle Leopold had insisted I get done in an expensive salon he also patronized. I assured myself that my travel companion must have noticed my wedding band. In fact, when I looked up and met his eyes, he inquired what I was doing in Europe or did I live here? That came as something of a relief, because it would let me explain the circumstances in greater detail, lest he get the wrong impression. Always apprehensive about how others are sizing me up, I have a never-ending need to explain myself to them. In this case, I felt there was a great deal to explain, and I resolved to deal with it honestly. I launched into a long and elaborate explanation about my impulsive initial questions, asking him to overlook my "forward" behavior. I mentioned that I was visiting my uncle, who was ill, and was compelled to speak our mother tongue, German, to him, then went on giving details of my personal visit with relatives in Zurich, where German again was the lingua franca. I wanted him to know how much I was yearning to get back to English after that, how very homesick for America and the English language I was.

The conversation got around to my uncle, and I told him about his illness and my concerns, but also about my hope for his recovery. "What rotten luck, poor girl! There you are in Paris, the most wonderful city in the world, stuck at your old uncle's sickbed." I quickly changed my tune, letting him know that Leopold was still rather active, that we were going out around town, taking in a lot Paris had to offer. He followed that with a remark about uncles that I didn't quite catch, so I came back with the details of Leopold's refurbishing a small château on the Marne. "Really! A château on the Marne—how extraordinary!" He repeated the word *château* in a sarcastic tone of voice. After that the conversation stalled for a while; finally, he inquired about my husband, giving me a chance to really let loose. I carried on about missing him and the baby, especially today, on my birthday, and how I was just dying to get back to Paris and from there back home. That got a reaction from him. "Your birthday!" He thought that called for a celebration, even some champagne. Meanwhile, I did tell him of my concern that my uncle might not have gotten my cable announcing my early arrival. That led to some banter about the unreliability of the French communications systems. Of course, I thought of every possibility, such as my uncle not having made it to his office today. Sometimes appointments such as those at the hospital, took priority over the office. "And Marcel isn't reliable either," I let on.

"Marcel? Who is he?"

"Oh, the chauffeur. Does only what he absolutely has to."

"Chauffeur," he repeated, a slight smile creeping over his face. Unperturbed, I went on to explain that even if Leopold hadn't gotten the message and I couldn't get out to the villa, I would always be able to stay in Paris overnight.

"Sensible solution," he allowed. I explained about the Hotel Calais, and how my uncle had a room at his disposal at any time. I thought it wise not to call it a suite, lest he take me as a four-flusher. I saw his lips curve into a smile, and he raised one eyebrow. I had the distinct feeling that he didn't believe one word of what I had been saying, and didn't quite know what to make of it.

The train was approaching the station in Paris, and that prompted me to get up impetuously. "Well, I'll soon find out," I tossed off.

I felt a hand on my shoulder, "What's the hurry? You certainly shouldn't be alone in Paris on your birthday!" The train having come to a halt, I made my way out, my companion following right behind me. To my immense joy and relief, I spotted Uncle Leopold only a short distance away on the platform. Next to him stood Marcel, uniformed and holding an enormous bouquet of pink roses in his hands. "Uncle Leopold!" I called out, and his arm went up in the air.

He strode quickly toward me, shouting, "Gerdele, you didn't think I would forget your birthday!" I looked over my shoulder for my English companion and saw him standing as if thunderstruck. I thought I heard him mutter something, but before I could introduce him, the crowd had swallowed him up.

OF COURSE, I WAS DELIGHTED TO SEE MY UNCLE, knowing that now I would not be alone on my birthday, but something about it surprised me. In fact, I hadn't expected him to remember my day. Caring and generous as he could be, remembering dates was not one of his strengths. Most evenings we would go out to dinner, and I guessed that tonight might be special, considering that he was aware of my birthday. As soon as Marcel settled us in the car, my enormous bouquet in my lap, I buried my face in the fragrant pink roses. "We're going to Maxim's," Uncle Leopold announced. "You know, it's the most—" I knew only too well, having read that it was the most famous, most elegant, most expensive restaurant in Paris. He didn't let me finish, so he was obviously glad that I knew of Maxim's renown. Nevertheless, he went on, "There will probably be a lot of prominent personalities at their usual tables. It could be anybody: famous film stars, English nobility, political figures, and other notables, so I would advise you not to gawk or, worse, ask for autographs. It wouldn't do, you know." He still treated me as if I were an uncouth child, and that irritated me. I inquired about mail, and it turned out that indeed there was a cable from Kurt. Now I realized how he had remembered my birthday. "You must be quite popular in America, because there are a number of envelopes as well."

Suddenly I lost any desire to go to Maxim's. All I could think of was getting my mail, but it would have been rude and ungrateful to back out. I tried another tack: "I have a great idea," I announced. "Why don't we have a simple dinner at home, just the two of us, and let's go to Maxim's tomorrow night. I'll be properly coiffed by then." I was thinking that then I could wear my one-shoulder black dress that even my uncle had approved of, though it had come off the rack back home. "Then you won't be ashamed of taking me to what must be the most elegant restaurant in Europe." For a while I thought he would go for it, but no, his mind was made up. It was to be Maxim's, and tonight.

Once we arrived, I tried to ignore the beautiful women in ravishing dresses and jewels, feeling totally out of my depth. I was sure we would be relegated to one of the more obscure tables, but no, we were actually seated in a most prominent spot, no doubt due to Leopold's lavish tip.

The waiter was ancient and looked like a tortoise, craning his neck over a stiff collar. My uncle appeared satisfied with the seating, and I tried to make sense of the enormous menu without making a fool of myself. I had to admit that I had never seen silver gleam as did this table setting, and I speculated aloud that in all likelihood the king of

England must have dined here and used the same fork, or had a drink from one of these very glasses. That pleased him, and he immersed himself in the selection of food—a ritual that took forever. Fortunately, he refrained from drinking wine or hard liquor, the only exception being champagne, which we would have with our dessert. I tried to rein in my normally huge appetite for the sake of good manners, having some vague idea that "ladies" were supposed to eat gingerly, always leaving some food on their plate.

With the order now resting in the waiter's capable hands, I had a chance to fill Leopold in on my mission to Switzerland. Still, I could barely concentrate on the details, my thoughts wandering to the cable that awaited me at his home, along with notes from other well-wishers. How unfortunate that Leopold had forgotten to bring the mail! I was sitting on a damask-covered banquette, the exquisite small lamp on the table throwing a warm, discreet light on the flawless table setting. The ultimate in understated elegance was all around me; waiters hovered silently, ready to anticipate our every whim.

I felt as if I were there in body only, chatting with as much animation as I could muster, while my thoughts were far away in Buffalo. They took me back to an upstairs apartment with modest furnishings, our first as newlyweds, the living room walls painted by us during one interminable night. I remembered how the paint had been a special bargain from Sears, Roebuck, and how we had gotten up earlier than usual, following our late-night labors, in order to inspect our handiwork. In the bright light of morning, Kurt could only pronounce the effect of the so-called pearl gray as "battleship gray." It was all there in my mind's eye, and beyond the dignified, elegant walls of Maxim's, I saw Vivie's high chair next to my silver-laden table, and I wanted so much to hear her innocent babble. Instead I went on praising the food and the decor, knowing how special they were. I was aware of how many people longed to be here just once in their lifetimes. Though I knew all that, and realized that I'd be spending a lot of time at home in years to come, I had the chance to be here just once, just now. Still, I would have liked nothing better than to be at home with my family. Finally the dessert came; it was soufflé au chocolat et Grand Marnier, along with champagne. We lifted our glasses, toasting my birthday and his health. I prayed for his recovery and included a silent toast to my family and the future.

He pulled a small package from his pocket. Once unwrapped, it proved to be a soft leather box. When I opened the lid, it revealed an exquisite cameo, magnificently framed in old gold relief, depicting in fine detail a scene from Greek mythology. Although I was ignorant of its rarity and value, my response exuded excitement and gratitude. These days the cameo reposes in my small jewelry box, together with other treasured mementos. It sits next to another precious, beloved birthday gift, also a brooch, made of colored toothpicks. On it, glued with meticulous care, is the word MOTHER spelled out in alphabet noodles. The O is a bit crooked and leans toward the T. It's a most treasured trinket my son, Jimmy, made in first grade in honor of a Mother's Day that fell on my birthday.

IN THE DAYS THAT FOLLOWED, Uncle Leopold began to feel the effects of the radiation treatments, although at first he tried valiantly to dismiss them. He was losing weight and tired easily. Once, after a particularly difficult treatment, I urged him to stay in Paris overnight, but he decided that despite the lateness of the hour and the long ride home, he wanted to go back to the country. It turned into a difficult drive. Some roads were closed, and the detours were endless. When we finally reached our destination, the house was hidden in darkness, only a feeble light glowing in the *porte cochère*. It all seemed so sad and doleful. I urged him to go up to his bedroom, but he expressed a desire for tea before retiring. I suggested that I would bring it to his room, but he resisted, preferring to remain downstairs. We made for the kitchen, that in itself being an unusual deviation from his regular routine. This took us through the dark salon and on to the dining room, where one lamp from the garden outside threw a shaft of light that eerily illuminated the long alabaster Italian Renaissance table slab, supported by kneeling female figures seemingly straining under the burden they were holding up. It was only a momentary glimpse, but it had aspects of a spectral scene. I quickly rushed ahead of him to the butler's pantry, adjacent to the kitchen. Someone

had left on the lights, the housekeeper and maid obviously having retired. With a sigh Uncle Leopold sat down on one of the stiff wooden
chairs in the pantry, and despite my repeated urgings that he go upstairs,
he wouldn't budge. He wanted to stay where he was, letting on that he
was cold. I put the kettle on the stove, saying that I would get him a
sweater. That took me upstairs along the grand curved staircase that
spiraled up four floors. His bedroom was on the second floor, and I made
for his dressing room, past the imposing rows of suits on oversized hang-
ers. Finding the shelf that held sweaters, I grabbed one that felt soft and
looked warm, then ran back downstairs. He was sitting on the hard chair
as I had left him, apparently too weak even to have taken off his jacket.
I proceeded to help him with what would normally have been a simple
routine task—removing the jacket and replacing it with the sweater. Then
I went to get the tea, pouring it into a heavy mug and adding several
sugar cubes and cream. That was the way he liked it, and I put the steam-
ing mug in front of him.

As he sipped his tea with a sigh of pleasure, his gaze wandered to his
left arm, and mine followed it. His shirtsleeve was protruding through a
gaping hole at the elbow of the sweater. I was about to say something,
but suddenly he put the mug down, lowered his head onto the table, and
began to weep. It was extremely painful to watch his uncontrollable
convulsions, cries of anguish emanating from his cancerous throat. I put
my arms around him, but that only made him cry harder. He motioned
me to sit down on the other chair, and when the sobs at last subsided, he
looked up, his eyes brimming with tears. His appearance had changed:
What I saw was an ill old man, his face showing an unhealthy pallor. I
was agitated, distraught, and quite frightened. Reaching for my hand
across the well scrubbed table, he whispered hoarsely, "That's really all I
ever wanted: a simple home, some hot tea, someone who cares."

I tried to calm him down, to reassure him, but he waved his hand in
a dismissive gesture. Sipping his tea again, he put his head back and
closed his eyes. I was looking at the crude mug on the plain table, taking
in the heavy cupboards on the wall, filled with Spode and Sèvres china.
Then my glance fell on the glass panel in the wall that showed CHAMBRE
DE MONSIEUR whenever the master of the house summoned a servant.
Through the door, I saw a section of the ghostly, empty dining room, and

the window that gave out on the parklike garden with its marble statuary. Then my gaze came back to my uncle, his arm in the torn sweater. Was that really all he ever wanted? A simple home, some hot tea? Of course not; that couldn't be so. No, he had chafed at the simple life as reflected in his childhood home, in which I also spent my childhood. The uneventful, slow pace of life in that environment was not for him. He always had had an urge to get away from that kind of bourgeois routine. For him there were distant, exotic, and glamorous places to be explored and conquered. Places such as I remembered seeing on his pigskin suitcases, colorful labels that gave off an aura of adventure, of sophistication: Hotel Baur au Lac, Zurich; Hotel Imperial, Wien; Lido, Venezia; Palace Hotel, Monte Carlo. I remembered how I had crouched near those suitcases, touching the labels from those far-off, glamorous places, wondering whether some day I, too, would see them. And how he, now a sick, old-looking man, had then sat cross-legged, dressed in boldly printed gold-and-blue silk pajamas, telling wondrous tales of his exploits. I remembered all the multistamped letters that had come over the years to his sister, still living in their childhood home, relating his travels. She was always the one to whom he turned to show his accomplishments. She would read and reread them at the window, between stitching a colorful tapestry with infinite patience. He himself would never have been happy within that confining frame of her life. He would have raged and fought as he did, and yet . . .

Had my mother been truly, absolutely happy and satisfied within the simple serenity of her milieu? I believe that that was the life that appealed to her. Was my uncle truly fulfilled by his success with women, money, and power? I think he was until his restlessness and ambition caught up with him, and it was only toward the end that he craved the world of stability he remembered from his childhood.

Almost a year later, I returned to his bedside before he died. We became very close during those final days and clung desperately to each other. Then he seemed to love me for myself, not as my mother's daughter, and he knew that I loved him. And when the inevitable happened, I tried to cope with my sorrow and pain. I had lost the last member of my immediate family.

Thinking back to that time, two nearly unrelated incidents that somehow typified his life come to mind. When we were looking for a cemetery, the undertaker told me that Père Lachaise in Paris, where he was to be buried, was *plus chic*, more *comme il faut* than the other burial places. Uncle Leopold would have approved. The other reflection somehow typifies his life for me. He, who had woven millions of miles of fabric on his hundreds of looms, was to have as his final covering a piece of black fabric, draped over the casket, and I spotted a hole in it. I am glad he could not see it, and it made me weep.

Now, more than half a century later, when I think of my uncle and my mother and my family's gene pool that I, too, have inherited, I am thinking of my uncle's constant drive to ever greater heights, some of which he conquered. But that leads me back to my mother's desire, which required only a peaceful life at home. I have never been driven to seek the limelight or, for that matter, recognition and fame, yet fate has catapulted me to some lofty places. Though I enjoyed them, I never craved a permanent foothold on those rarefied heights. My mother's genes must be dominant, then, and for that I am grateful.

Inside the Château on the Marne

Coincidence

1960s, BUFFALO, NEW YORK; 1999, SYDNEY, AUSTRALIA

*T*HE DOORBELL RANG, AND THE MAILMAN HANDED ME a square, battered, ungainly parcel tied with heavy twine. He tried to wipe particles of ice from his glove to hand me a pen, so I could sign the receipt that was fluttering furiously in his grasp. That accomplished, I quickly shut the door, warmth enveloping me again as I walked into the kitchen, where I put the package on the counter, brushing off the snow that was turning into rivulets of water and dirt. My name and address were nearly illegible, now that the ink was running on the carton. Rows of foreign stamps protruded from under the heavy knotted cord. It had arrived from Vienna, Austria, and my mother's cousin Pepi had sent it. While undoing the tangle of twine, I recalled what my distant cousin had written a few months ago.

Pepi had been visiting Bielsko, or Bielitz, as we still called it, dating back to the time when it had been part of the Austro-Hungarian Empire. All of us who had grown up speaking German tended to forget the fact that the town had been ceded to Poland after World War I. Our large extended family had lived there for generations, but no one was left now. Pepi and her brother were the only members of my immediate family who had survived the Holocaust, she having escaped to Siberia. Her brother, Alfred, or Bubi, as he was affectionately known, had been an officer in the Polish army, was taken prisoner by the Germans, but somehow survived the war in Hungary. Both brother and sister had settled in Vienna after World War II. It was from there that Pepi had made the pilgrimage to our hometown in order to visit the cemetery. She had hoped to find her father's grave, along with those of other family members fortunate enough to have died a natural death before the war. On their way to the cemetery, located in the vicinity of my childhood home, a woman approached her, inquiring whether she was by chance related to my family. The woman had recognized Pepi by her beautiful bright red hair. That established, she let on to Pepi that there were photographs in her possession that belonged to my family. Confirming the fact that my family was gone, Pepi noted that I had survived and was living in the United States. To her surprise, that message did not seem to elicit a joyous response. Pepi assured the woman how grateful I would be that she had preserved those precious mementos, but the woman insisted on anonymity. She would not divulge her name or how she had come into possession of the photos. Rather, she suggested that Pepi should send them on to me. She herself wanted no direct contact with me. Puzzled as my cousin was by the encounter, I was equally surprised and thought of it intermittently, but as time elapsed, I had half forgotten the incident.

Impatiently and beset by a host of questions, I tore off the paper, opened the box, and carried it to the living room. There I sat on the floor and poured the entire contents onto the carpet. They came tumbling out in a rushing torrent from the dim interior of the box in which they had been tightly packed. Here were what seemed like hundreds of images of my family members, setting off a turmoil of recollections. My mind became a jumble of memories, more than I could coherently absorb at that moment, leading to a rush of searching questions. I sat mute, stunned by what I was finding, looking into the box for a word, a clue. Gradually the pieces of the puzzle began to fall into place. At the very bottom, caught in a glued strip of paper, I got a glimpse of a familiar sight, and reached for it in awe and disbelief. It felt icy cold to the touch. On it I traced my father's name, engraved on its mother-of-pearl surface. When I turned it over, there was a Hebrew inscription: *Shabat Kodesh*, Holy Sabbath. My father had held this knife in his hand every Friday night when he cut the challah, the traditional Sabbath bread. Then Papa would recite the familiar benediction that marked the beginning of the day of rest. To think that this had been held by Papa's hand at its last use! Reverently I lifted it to my lips, thankful that it had come back to me in such miraculous fashion. Outside, icy snow mixed with rain was beating against my living room picture window. I looked at the snow-covered evergreens, whipped by the wind; at my children's ice-encrusted swings; their playhouse roof, piled high with snow. And I was holding in my hand something my father had touched.

Now I was back there, back in my childhood. It suddenly came to me to whom we had entrusted the treasure that lay in front of me. Her name was Jadwiga. A handsome, large, buxom woman with blond hair gathered into a heavy coil at the nape of her neck. The German occupation of Poland was becoming ever more oppressive for Jews, and there had been several official announcements that we were to be "resettled" elsewhere. It meant we would be taken to an unknown destination on one of those horrible transports that spelled complete uncertainty as to our ultimate fate. The orders had been rescinded several times after each member of the Jewish community paid his or her share of the heavy "fines" that were levied against them. This was just another of the Nazis' subterfuges, by which they extracted every last piece of jewelry or money from their hapless victims.

Jadwiga was in a state of high excitement when she confided to my mother what she had learned from a reliable source, namely that "good" furniture, paintings, and other valuables would shortly be taken from Jews. She assured Mama that if we had anything that my parents wanted to hold on to for special reasons, she would be glad to take it for safekeeping until after the war. Of course, we had long before sold most of our belongings of value in order to obtain food or to pay the dreaded penalties, but there were still a few things left. One was a long credenza that had stood in the dining room. It consisted of several sections, each in a different wood, beautifully carved and linked by an intricate design. We also had a treasured painting by the French painter Dornée, as well as a few vases and bowls of sentimental value to my mother because they had been in the family for generations.

Jadwiga knew someone with a horse and wagon—cars or trucks no longer being available to Jews—who would transport the pieces to her spacious home. I believe that the wagon pulled up in front of our house a day or two later, and I was helping with the loading of those last few pieces, feeling sad at having to part with them. Mama was certain, she said, that we would see them again, hopefully soon. A few days later I was dispatched to Jadwiga's home on an errand I can no longer recall, but I do remember my surprise at finding the woman's home filled with precious possessions from Jewish homes all around town. The far-left section of our sideboard had three gray, felt-lined drawers in which Mama had kept the antique silver tableware that had been in the family for generations. There were only a few very old pieces left, and they were in the upper drawer, together with Papa's Sabbath knife. The right section housed several large velvet-covered photograph albums. I remembered how, when I had been confined to bed with a childhood illness, I would be allowed to look through albums as a means of distraction. That privilege always came with the admonition to be careful not to spill food or drink on them.

Now, decades later in my new life, I gathered what must have happened. Jadwiga removed our photos from the albums so she could use them for herself. She also discarded the knife because it had Hebrew text on it and was of no use to her, then dumped it all into a cardboard box. The question arose: Why did she keep it? Originally, perhaps, because she thought that some member of our family might come back. No doubt she forgot about it over the years. When no one returned to claim any of it, it must have reposed in some dark corner of her attic or basement, until the encounter with Pepi rekindled the memory of the circumstances with vague pangs of conscience. It would be safe to give it to this member of our family, who knew nothing of the other objects in her safekeeping.

With trembling hands, I spread out the pictures on the floor and studied the faces that were staring at me. How I wished they were alive so that I might embrace them. Here was the only tangible proof left that they had ever existed. They were the features of those murdered in cold blood, as they had looked in their ordinary lives. To think that those images had sat in a dark, airless box in the home of a stranger for more than twenty years, waiting to be "liberated" as their flesh-and-blood counterparts had never been. From there, they had been taken to Vienna, where the box, securely tied with heavy cord, insured for ten dollars, made its voyage across the Atlantic Ocean in the hold of a ship that eventually docked in New York. From there, it had made the trek across New York State, and on a bitter February day arrived in Buffalo, at the home of the only person on earth who knew the name of every person in those pictures. There they were, resplendent in their finery, with serious faces, awaiting the click that would etch their images on glass plates or film as a permanent record of their existence. But what if they had not reached me through this most fortuitous set of circumstances? Their likenesses and identities could have been lost forever, had the ink on the package been further blurred by the elements before it could be delivered to me.

In their formal poses, men stood rigid against the photographer's props of garden gates and potted palms, their watch chains visible from their vest and pockets, spanning their portly bellies. Omama, my maternal grandmother, her ample bosom tightly laced into a gown with leg-o'-mutton sleeves, followed the etiquette of the time to appear unsmiling, even on her engagement picture. For his part, Grandfather, whom I remember only dimly, sported an elegant cravat and spectacles, necessary because he was nearsighted. Those must have been the very glasses that had been instrumental in bringing about the marriage.

GROWING UP, I WAS ALWAYS CURIOUS to listen to all the tales floating around in adult conversations. Yes, the matchmaker was a woman who, like so many others in our town frequented my great-grandparents' store. Bielsko was involved in the production and sales of textiles. My great-grandparents had a large, fine store on the Ringplatz, the town square, in which their five sons worked as a matter of course. It was only their daughter, Rosa, who was spared the store experience. Apparently a match was being arranged between my grandparents when rumor reached my grandmother and her family that the young man in question was nearly blind. The crafty matchmaker promptly went to look for young Jakob Mückenbrunn and slyly asked him the time. He pulled out his watch and gave the correct answer. The wise matchmaker wanted to make absolutely sure, saying that she had set her watch by the clock of the church tower on the town square. Could he check it out? So young Jakob went outside, squinted toward the church tower and gave the correct time, and that clinched his marriage to Julie Getreider. With the benefit of 20/20 hindsight, I came to the conclusion that my grandfather's poor eyesight might have been a blessing. He was very handsome, while grandmother could hardly have been counted among the town's beauties.

Almost every picture brought back a memory, a tale, a saying. On one of them was a photograph of Tante Sala with my mother, as they were comfortably settled in an outrageous contraption of an airplane, with weights and a pendulum reminiscent of those on grandfather clocks. Of course, it was common knowledge in the family that Aunt Sala never traveled; she was hard of hearing and afraid of leaving the confines of Bielitz. It was rumored that her husband had married her only for her large dowry.

I found myself randomly sifting through school pictures, baby pictures, one of me lying in a carriage with starched curtains, no particular expression on my face. My brother, Artur, then five years old, appeared to be staring at me, uncertain whether to smile or cry. The way he put it to me later was that he was merely following the prompt to smile for the photo, while in reality he should have been crying in despair at the "pest" of a sister who had recently arrived.

Memory after memory washed over me, staining my face with tears, tears of joy and pain. Here was Papa, tall, slim, handsome in the uniform of an Austrian officer, his hand resting on the hilt of his saber, his face reflecting a look of confidence about all that lay ahead. He met my mother in the course of searching for quarters for his military unit, and became interested in that household because he had spotted my mother. When Grandmother told him there was no room in their home, he returned undaunted the next day, carrying white lilacs—out of season—not for my mother, but wisely for my grandmother. Papa always knew how to handle my imperious grandmother. It took only a few months until the couple became engaged, their plans being to get married as soon as the war was over.

Whenever Papa wanted to tease my mother, he would tell the story about the end of the war, after the armistice was announced. Mama allegedly sent him—her soldier-fiancé—a cable informing him of the end of hostilities in case he was not aware of events. Mama never denied the story. She would dismiss it by saying that she had merely wanted to convey her joy to him that the war was finally over. But those who knew my mother believed Papa's version, and there was always a great deal of teasing about it. Among the photos were some old school friends of Mama's, with flowery dedications of unwavering friendship and devotion penned on the reverse sides. One struck me as particularly painful in light of what was to happen later. The young man who had declared his "eternal" friendship had turned into the man who became one of the town's staunchest Nazis after the German invasion. What was particularly hurtful was Mama's encounter with him on the street during those early days after the takeover, an occasion when he looked straight past her as though she were a complete stranger.

Next Erwin's picture leaped out at me. Erwin Schreier, on whom I had had a teenage crush. Now, decades later, I saw how very handsome he really had been. He was my mother's cousin, the eldest son of Tante Rosa, my grandfather's sister. Her husband was Onkel Viktor. They were the wealthy branch of our family, owning two men's ready-to-wear stores and living in grand style in the most fashionable part of town, where they occupied an entire floor of a building. Tante Rosa and Onkel Viktor had seven children. First came four boys, followed by three girls. After Erwin came Oskar, dubbed "the Good." He owned a car and usually drove the aunts to their various destinations. Erwin and Oskar owned the finest men's store in town, on Third of May Street, Bielsko's most prominent business street. The store, which was called Gentlemen, carried fine English suits as well as expensive ties from France. Artur, the third son, worked alternately in his parents' and his brothers' stores. Moritz, the youngest, was considered the handsomest bachelor in our social circles. He had two interests at which he excelled: tennis and dancing. Pursuing one of those activities, he met a young woman in Warsaw, who came from a very wealthy intellectual family. In keeping with the emphasis the family placed on a good education, Regina had attended a finishing school in Switzerland. I only crossed paths with Regina once, shortly after her marriage to Moritz, when they paid a visit to Bielsko. She was a stunning redhead, and they made a handsome, exotic, sophisticated couple. They had a daughter, an event that caused a great deal of rejoicing within the family. It was Tante Rosa and Onkel Viktor's first and only grandchild, but her name turned out to present a problem. She was named Christina, the diminutive being Krysia. Not only was that a totally Christian name, but because her grandparents spoke only German, they were unable to pronounce the child's name properly. Nevertheless, she was the darling of the family.

Of my uncle and aunt's three daughters, Bertha was the oldest. She was a quiet, introspective young woman, immersed in books most of the time. Everybody hoped she would marry a young man who was then completing his medical studies. Minna, the next in line, was a total contrast to her sister: blond, blue-eyed, vivacious, and an excellent dancer and skier. She later married an equally fun-loving young attorney before the outbreak of the war. I remember it as a grand wedding, and their dilemma was: Should they spend their honeymoon in Paris, where some international exposition was being held at the time, or should they use the fund to furnish their apartment? Endless family discussions ensued on the subject of the choices open to them. Most of them were critical of their option for Paris; it would be a frivolous and not at all prudent thing to do. So they stayed at home, were furnishing their apartment and getting ready to throw a lavish party, when there were ominous signs that war might break out. That threat becoming more real with the passing of each day, the entire family fled to the interior of Poland, hoping to evade the German army should it cross into Poland from nearby occupied Czechoslovakia, where German troops were reported to be massing. That meant that my immediate family—parents, brother, and I—were the only ones left in town, because my father had had a heart attack approximately three weeks earlier.

It took the Germans less than two weeks to occupy Poland, and a few relatives came straggling back from the interior, among them Erwin, who told us that he was going to the German authorities to get the keys to his store. My father strongly advised against such a foolhardy step, but Erwin was determined to go. He never returned, but a few weeks later a small square box arrived at our home with a brief note attached, informing us that Erwin had died in Buchenwald of "pneumonia," a

Nazi euphemism for their merciless killings in concentration camps. The box contained his ashes. (This was a "courtesy" that shortly thereafter was discontinued.) I sobbed uncontrollably, remembering how handsome he had been, how gentle to me. Whenever I had stopped by his store, he would take me to the *Italiener*, the Italian ice cream vendor, for a special treat. It came back to me how one day I had stood with him and watched a painter laboring on the sign that hung over the entrance to his store. GENTLEMEN was emblazoned on it in large maroon letters, bordered by gold, and Erwin had explained that the word meant *Herren* but more so—men of noble bearing. "Someone like you, Erwin," I had responded, after which he put his arms around me and smiled. Erwin, the quintessential gentle man.

As I looked at the photograph on the living room floor in Buffalo, I thought of Erwin—his photograph still conveying elegance after so many years—and the first of our family to die in a concentration camp. To think that Erwin, or rather tangible proof of his existence, was lying before me now in my new life.

My gaze wandered to the next photo: Aunt Mania, wearing a fashionable Persian lamb coat holding her infant son in her arms. Beautiful Aunt Mania, of whose husband it was said that he spent too many hours in coffeehouses. In my naïveté, I had wondered what Uncle Josef was doing wrong, and what was so odious about a café?

Now here was a class picture that went back to my grammar school days. Before that moment, I could have sworn I would never remember most of the names of my classmates, yet it was as though a curtain had lifted, I was back in school, and all the kids' names sprang to mind. In vivid detail I could recall their voices, their inflections, their idiosyncratic speech, the color of their dress, despite the fact that the photo was in black and white.

Next my paternal grandfather's face stared at me, and a wave of nostalgia swept over me. Here he was, his kind eyes seeming to scrutinize me, his white beard adding an aura of dignity to his countenance. He had died shortly after I was born; yet, growing up, I had felt I knew him. Tales of his Spartan self-discipline when it came to his own life, his deep understanding of human nature, his compassion and love for his fellow humans, and his indulgence when it came to others' failings were legendary within the family. They became the cornerstone of my own beliefs, imparting much that would stand me in good stead when coping with the vicissitudes of life later on. I couldn't help but muse that my childhood concept of what God must look like had perhaps not been too misguided when I pictured him much like the face I was regarding now.

Partially obscured by Grandfather's photo, Grandmother's likeness came into view. Nechama (her name meaning "comfort" in Hebrew) was a tiny woman, frail, her face wizened like a shriveled winter apple from our vegetable cellar. I loved her a great deal, and although I would never have admitted it to anyone, preferred her to my Omama, my maternal grandmother, whom I saw on a daily basis and who indulged her only grandchildren, Artur and me, to the extent of spoiling us far beyond our parents' wishes. What came into focus with Grandmother was that one summer she taught me how to crack pumpkin seeds between my teeth, blowing the shells into the wind and savoring the delicious taste of the kernels. Visiting my father's mother in Czortkov (now in Ukraine), a town that seemed to me to have retained its medieval character, was to give me an understanding of Marc Chagall's depiction of his hometown, Vitebsk, once I became familiar with that artist's paintings later in life. I could identify with the ancient lopsided houses, horses leaping over their rooftops, with sunflowers grotesquely taller than the homes in whose gardens they grew. Czortkov was like that, and had many attractions for a young child.

I still have "sweet" memories of an almost daily ritual, that of Grandmother shelling out five *groszy* so that I could buy my favorite, a large chocolate square wrapped in colorful foil. I was determined to collect all the available colors in the course of my stay and decided to stash away those wrappers in Grandmother's prayer book. One of her neighbors chanced to come by, catching me in the act of smoothing my colorful hoard between the *tefilla*'s pages. She took me severely to task for daring to be disrespectful to God's book, in her words a "sin" and an "abomination." Taken aback by such censure, I was upset, pangs of conscience overtaking me for all I had done wrong. Grandmother was just coming into the room, having overheard some of the stern lecture, and, like a tigress, immediately leaped to my defense. I remember some of her argument. God, she declared, having to observe all the terrible things people in this realm do, must be delighted with the pretty wrappers in His book, put there by a well-meaning child. After which she promptly gave me another coin to buy more sweets and wrappers. Looking at her wrinkled face now, no longer her young granddaughter but a mother of three children myself, I remembered that during the hours of labor before the births of my children, I had been thinking of her. How she must have wept in anguish over the loss of the first five of her ten children, those who had died in infancy in that primitive environment. "I love children so much," she had told me, gently touching my bangs and kissing my cheek. She had had so many children and grandchildren, but of all of them I was the only one to survive the Holocaust. I kissed her picture, held it close, and began to weep.

The light in the room grew dimmer, and the wind outside was subsiding. It was gradually getting darker in the early dusk of winter's afternoon, and my reveries were interrupted by the chiming of the doorbell. That got me to my feet fast, and mechanically I switched on the light, then went to open the door. It was the kids coming home from school, their faces flushed from the cold, their voices exuberant as usual. Quickly the atmosphere changed to chatter and laughter, to breathless tales of the day's happenings in school, and it wasn't long before the smell of cinnamon toast and cocoa permeated the air. Taking Vivie, Leslie, and Jimmy into the living room, I tried to explain the treasure that had arrived that day and the personalities behind those strange faces. But how to pin down their idiosyncrasies, their hopes, their dreams, their disappointments? And most of all, how to explain their ultimate fate?

Pointing from aunts and uncles to cousins, I told them how most of them were in the habit of visiting us during those fondly remembered golden Sunday afternoons, for they all thought of our house as their ancestral home. It so happened that both of my grandparents were the oldest among their siblings, and so they and we were the only ones still living in what had been the central family home for a couple of generations. Our location was considered a bit remote, though, for it lay on the outskirts of town, whereas most of them lived in larger, more modern apartments, some in beautiful villas. But Sundays would see them assembled in our home, my aunts making themselves more *bequem* (comfortable) by removing their corsets, while the men would loosen their ties. I remember that we, the children, would engage in typically rambunctious behavior, excitedly racing around, trying to catch a ball and tag one another.

Those warm, sunlit afternoons, the fragrance of coffee and vanilla wafting through the house, conjured up visions of fine porcelain cups, holding that strong brew, topped by billows of whipped cream, while we would wash down the sweets with lemonade. Of course, there would be coffeecakes or seasonal fruitcakes and a variety of cookies that we eagerly devoured. Among the grownups, all the joys and cares of the past week were put on the table in a sort of group therapy session; confidences were exchanged, gossip shared. And I, curious brat that I was, would always eavesdrop on the adult conversation, eager to pick up bits of revelations not meant for my ears, catching more than the grownups ever believed I could understand.

I decided to leave the pictures on the living room carpet until Kurt's return from the office, at which point I went over the stories again, unable to separate myself from myriad images. All around me were my family and the recollections they evoked, each dear and special, and for awhile I could delude myself that they had come back and we were reunited.

My first impulse was to express my thanks to Jadwiga, despite the fact that she obviously had declined any contact with me, but Kurt emphatically dissuaded me from my impetuous resolve. He patiently explained how I would only embarrass her, that she clearly wanted to keep her identity a secret, that quite likely she didn't want me to inquire about the other, more materially valuable possessions that had been entrusted to her. He reasoned that she had saved the greatest treasure I could have hoped for, and I saw the logic of it. It was sound advice, and I never got in touch with her. Yet I often wondered about and marveled at the incredible coincidence that had brought those treasured photos back to me. What chance was there that Pepi should have decided to visit her hometown on that particular day? I was to find out subsequently that she did so only once in more than twenty years. And what did it take during that relatively short walk to the cemetery for Jadwiga to pass her, recognize her by her flaming red hair, and make up her mind to offer the box of photos? And that those photos would reach me, the only person in the world still alive who could identify all the faces frozen in time?

Coincidence?

MORE THAN THREE DECADES AFTER I WAS REUNITED WITH THE PHOTOGRAPHS from my youth, Kurt and I were visiting Sydney, Australia. Much to my delight I had found that several people, acquaintances from my hometown, had made their way to Australia after the war. Some had survived in Russia, two had escaped to China, and another was one of my schoolmates whose family had vacationed in England during that fateful summer of 1939 and had wisely never returned to Poland. She wanted us to meet a few others from Bielsko. Altogether we were sixteen people at tea that afternoon. It was a balmy October day during what was spring in Australia. My schoolmate, whom I remembered as a tall, willowy, long-legged girl of fifteen, was now a gray-haired woman in her seventies. Here was an assembly of people, not all of whom I had known, but all speaking with accents and voice modulations so similar to mine. Tables were set in the lovely garden, in the shade of trees; once again the scents of vanilla and cinnamon pervaded the air. Here were cakes and cookies in shapes I remembered so well but had not seen in many decades. I allowed myself to inhale those familiar fragrances and to luxuriate in the memory of those warm, carefree, golden, seemingly safe summer afternoons. A longed for homeyness enveloped me once again. I wanted to be quiet and just listen to the lilt in the voices around me, taking in the scent of memory. Yet time and again, there were questions relating to something topical, to which I had to respond. Intermittently I was able to close my eyes for a few seconds, jealously guarding the bliss that was mine.

Then I sat bolt upright. Had I heard those words? Had someone at the far table mentioned that name? I quickly went over to the table. "Did I hear you say 'Moritz Schreier'?"

"Why, yes. Why do you ask?" the question came from a woman I had not known before, and she continued, "How do you know him?"

"He was my mother's first cousin; do you know what happened to him?" She gestured for me to sit down and said haltingly, "Unfortunately,

I do. Moritz was killed in Auschwitz early in the war." A bee was buzzing around, settling on the golden rim of the cake plate. The dreaded word burst into the serenity of the hour.

"How do you know that?" I asked mechanically.

"Regina, his wife, told me." She brushed the bee away.

"Were you in some camp with Regina?"

"Why, no, I met Regina after the war here in Sydney." Regina, here in Sydney!

"Regina survived?" I was incredulous, full of questions, and she proceeded to tell the story.

Early during the war, Regina and Moritz had been forced to live in the Warsaw Ghetto, but Moritz was soon picked up and sent to Auschwitz. In the years that followed, Regina survived against incredible odds, mostly through the efforts of a kind, resourceful man whom she ultimately married once the war was over. Eventually, they emigrated to Australia and made a new life. Unfortunately, she was no longer alive when I visited Sydney. Regina, beautiful Regina, and Moritz. What a stunning couple they had been! How they had loved to play tennis and go dancing. Through the babble of voices around me, I held fast to my memories of them and of the Schreier family—Tante Rosa, Onkl Viktor, Erwin, Oskar, and Moritz, the accomplished dancer. Something in my subconscious kept nagging at me, something about a Polish name that Tante Rosa and Onkel Viktor could never properly pronounce. Yes, it was the name of their only grandchild, Krysia. She was Moritz and Regina's baby daughter. Even in my half-formed thoughts, I avoided the mention of the youngest family member, knowing what had happened to Jewish babies in Nazi Germany and the Warsaw Ghetto. But her picture was still imprinted on my mind. Beautiful baby Krysia, in her proud grandparents' arms. Impulsively, I blurted out, "They had a child, a little girl named Krysia." I was not expecting an answer.

"Why, yes, Krysia lives here." It was a matter-of-fact statement.

"Krysia here?" I was stunned.

And the story unfolded further. Because she came from a very wealthy family, Regina succeeded in smuggling Krysia out of the ghetto, and once the deportation was announced, she had made sure to hide a great number of jewels on her to meet any contingency. She also managed to get a

Polish family who lived in the countryside to take in her baby daughter. The family to whom Krysia was entrusted had a son, somewhat older than Krysia, who became her devoted "brother." During her stay, she was treated with care and love, and it was only with great reluctance that the family gave up the child to her natural mother at the end of the war. Regina's husband adopted Krysia, and she grew up in Sydney. She remained an only child and was greatly devoted to her father, who doted on her. Shortly before Regina's death, her husband implored her to tell Krysia that he was not her biological father, something that Regina reluctantly consented to do. In the end, she disclosed only a minimum of information: Krysia's father's name and birthplace but scarcely anything else. I sat speechless. To think that Krysia had survived and was living here in Sydney! What an unlikely scenario.

"Oh, how I would love to see her!"

"Well, that can be arranged. Let me give you her phone number. Call her." How nonchalantly those words were spoken. That's when I panicked. Should I do it? Should I destroy the serenity Krysia might have found in the love of the man who brought her up, the only father she knew and adored? Would I bring chaos into her life? Would it be kinder not to say anything, just to rejoice in the knowledge that the most unlikely member of the entire Schreier family had survived? But soon my selfishness took over. I wanted to see her; I wanted to touch her, to embrace a member of my lost family. My informant readily agreed to establish the initial contact and put the news to Krysia as gently as possible. She would convey my hope and desire to see her.

FROM THEN THE HOURS SEEMED ENDLESS. I could think of nothing else. Finally, the long-awaited phone call came. It took no time until Krysia and her handsome husband, Dany, sat across from us in our hotel room

She is blond, beautiful, and exudes intelligence. She is a lawyer. When she speaks, and in the way she moves her lips, she is the image of her grandmother. She knew nothing of her father's family. She has only one photograph that her mother gave her: her father in half-profile. She can hardly make out his face. She plied me with endless questions, and I told her about her grandparents and her uncles: Erwin, Oskar, and Artur. Also about her aunts: Berta, Minna, and Klara. I remembered that I had a photograph in my possession, back home in the United States, on which her grandparents hold her in their arms. Blessedly, on that day so long ago when Pepi went to Bielitz from Vienna, Jadwiga recognized her, and the photos that only I could completely identify came into my possession. I reminisced for hours about family lore, and we promised to see each other again soon. It was no empty promise either, for she and Dany were to come to a family event the following year—the bat mitzvah of my granddaughter Jessica Simon.

Once we returned from our trip, I found the picture I had remembered and forwarded it to Krysia. On the back, in my childish scrawl, I had written so long ago, "*Onkel Viktor and Tante Rosa mit der Krysia*" (Uncle Viktor and Aunt Rosa with Krysia).

I've heard it said that "coincidence is God's way of remaining anonymous."*

Krysia with her parents

---

* While I was writing this story, we had an e-mail from Krysia and Dany, announcing their impending second visit to us.

Homecoming

DECEMBER 1975, BUFFALO, NEW YORK

IT HAD BEEN SNOWING RELENTLESSLY FOR A COUPLE OF DAYS, and the extended weather forecast was equally bleak. More snow and hazardous driving conditions could be expected. Motorists were advised to use extreme caution; part of the New York State Thruway might be closed.

Our son, Jimmy, a freshman at Tufts University, called to check in. Two of his closest friends from Buffalo, David and Kevin, had driven to Boston following their exams, and the three of them would be spending a few days there before all returned to Buffalo for winter break. "We should be home on Tuesday," Jimmy said, adding, "in time for dinner."

"Drive carefully," we admonished. "Go slowly; take care."

"We will; don't worry, Mom."

On Monday, before going to bed, I suggested that we should perhaps leave the front door unlocked. You never knew, perhaps Jimmy might make it home earlier. "He told you it'll be tomorrow, in time for dinner, and he does have a key. Why do you always . . ." was Kurt's predictable response.

"Yes, I know." I was halfway up the stairs when I quietly went down again, unlocked the door, put the porch light on, and noticed that it was still snowing hard. It took me a long time to fall asleep, but suddenly I awoke, not knowing what time it was. Kurt was up at the same instant. Our bedroom door opened and a voice, tinged with emotion, whispered, "Can you use a son a day earlier?"

I glanced at the clock—it was four in the morning. We followed him to his room, helping him carry a pile of books and a huge duffel bag that

I surmised contained dirty laundry. He looked around, fixing his gaze on an object on the wall over his bed, where a large plastic perpetual calendar hung. When he was still at home, every morning he had religiously moved the white ring that fit over the blue plastic pegs to the proper date. The ring remained where he had left it when he went off to college. "My God," he exclaimed, "I haven't been here since the second of September!" When he said that, an invisible curtain parted for me, taking me back to another September 2, long, long before. I had carried within me a dream that was tied to that day. On that day, more than thirty-five years later, Jimmy had fulfilled that dream.

The joy of his homecoming filled us with exuberance, and I couldn't let go of him. No, he wasn't hungry, he assured us, but very tired after the long drive on slippery roads through blinding snow. After we returned to our room, I noticed that his light stayed on for a while. So I went back and found him lying in bed reading. The room that had been so quiet, so orderly for the past few months, now seemed full of life. His duffel bag leaned against his desk, a blue sweater protruded from it, and his shoes lay at odd angles on the floor.

He was back—thank God, he was back. His cheeks were still red from the cold outside; his light brown hair was tousled, curling over his forehead. He lay stretched out under his blanket; he seemed taller than when he left. "It's good to be home," he said. I kissed him and turned off his light.

I went back to bed, holding on to this moment, so special, so moving, so exalted, which held the fulfillment of my own dream. I thought of that other September 2 when I was fifteen . . . September 1939. It was a beautiful day, and my childhood garden was bursting with brilliant flowers. The trees in the orchard hung heavy with fruit. I was ready to start school, but that had been suspended the day before, when Germany invaded Poland. On September 2, a Saturday, suddenly all power was shut off. The lights, the radio—nothing worked. There was a deceptive calm in the air. How peaceful the old house in which I had been born seemed. I had mused that surely nothing evil would ever be able to penetrate those thick, safe walls. We were cut off from the world, cut off from the voices on the radio, but we were safe together: my parents, my brother, and I.

On the morning of September 3—the day Britain and France declared war on Germany—Nazi hordes burst into our town, brutally shattering the life I had known and loved. Soon all that was gone. That's when my dream was born, the dream of a return. Innumerable times during the war years I harked back to the memory of that last, peaceful Saturday of my childhood. The thought of a return to those carefree days nourished me during my darkest hours. When life became nearly intolerable, that dream gave me the strength to endure. As time went on, the dream of my homecoming became keener. In my imagination I played with the fragments of that dream. I always wished that I would be the last one in my family to return home, and to find my parents and my brother already there. Sometimes in my mind, I would deliberately prolong the agony by returning home without entering it. In my mind I would envision coming home during the night and not waking my parents, but choosing, instead, to wait in the garden for the first rays of the sun.

Of course, I knew my impetuous nature better than that, realizing that I would never be able to wait, that I would storm into the house, wake my parents, and tell them that I was back, that I had come home.

It was not to be. But Jimmy's homecoming, playing out many of the details of those dreams that were harbored during many bitter years, helped assuage my anguish. For the first time, I no longer felt quite the same sharp edge of pain that I never went home. As long as my son did, and found his parents where he had left them and his boyhood room unchanged, something vital was restored.

KURT WAS FAST ASLEEP. I walked to the window, opened the drapes, and watched the steadily falling snow. Memories swept over me. Memories of the joy, fulfillment, and healing that my children have given me. Thinking of Jimmy, I had sensed that somehow he would try to get home earlier; that in all probability, he was already on his way when he called. Since childhood, Jimmy and his sisters, Vivie and Leslie, have always tried to save us from needless worry. Jimmy knew that if he was really coming back on Tuesday evening, the bad weather and the uncertainty over the driving conditions would cause us concern until he arrived home. It took me back to the time when he was a little boy away in summer camp, and I had taken the responsibility of caring for a goldfish he had named Moses. It was only right, he thought, to give him that name because, like the biblical Moses, the fish had been "drawn forth from the water"—albeit at a school fair.

Unfortunately, one morning I found Moses belly up in the goldfish bowl. There was nothing else to do but go out and try to find a double for Moses. Realizing, however, that Jimmy was better acquainted with Moses than I, I wrote to him—cleverly, I thought—that someone I knew had given me a tip on a new, more nutritious fish food than the one we were using. It appeared to be doing wonders, because Moses was really thriving on it.

Back from summer camp, Jimmy thanked me for taking such good care of Moses. It was only many years later, while talking about fish stories, that he informed me that when he returned from camp and saw the replacement goldfish, he figured out my ruse. Earlier still, when Jimmy was five, we spent part of the summer at a Canadian beach. I have tender memories of a starlit sky, over which hung a huge August moon. He was with his sisters when they spotted it. They would fetch us from the cottage, they said, so we could also enjoy seeing it. They told him to hold the moon until we came. I can still see him, stretching out his little arms to an elusive moon in an attempt to hold it for us.

The memory of that summer also brings back an early sign of his character, so much in evidence today. He and his friend Andy had found a few small tadpoles, and each of the boys made a small pond. There was also a dam, made of stones, shells, and seaweed, in which to confine the tiny creatures. One morning Jimmy came back from the beach, his huge blue eyes brimming with tears. At first he refused to tell us the reason for his agitation, but eventually he broke down and blurted out that that morning he had felt so sorry for the tadpoles that he had decided to release them. I could only praise him for that life-saving act, which seemed to calm him down a bit, but that was not the reason for his upset. He was facing a dilemma. He had freed Andy's tadpoles as well! Did he have the right to do so? When I asked why he hadn't consulted Andy before granting the tadpoles their freedom, his argument was that Andy probably would not have agreed to restore the tadpoles to Lake Erie. That was not enough, however. The next question was one of morality. Who had greater rights: the tadpoles or Andy? Right then and there, I realized that when he grew up, he would probably become a lawyer, which is exactly what he did.

A CERTAIN CRAFTINESS AND INSIGHT INTO MY METHODS OF UPBRINGING manifested themselves early as well. One afternoon I was informed by a "reliable source" that Jimmy had picked up a half-smoked cigarette on the sidewalk while the kids were playing outside and he had smoked it. Since the reliable source was Jimmy's older sister Leslie, who was typically protective of him, I knew the report was true. That night at dinner, Kurt and I confronted Jimmy with the allegation. At first he tried to wriggle out of the situation by denying it, which really got me going. When he finally admitted his misdeed, we told him that the punishment would be severe. It wasn't so much that he had smoked the cigarette, but that he had lied to us. He wouldn't be able to watch TV for a month. As soon as I cooled off, I realized that the penalty was far too severe, but felt I could not just change my mind without a good reason. I have always emphasized to my children that they could come to me with any problem and I would lend a willing ear. But lying was not acceptable. I was caught now, and truly sorry for having acted so rashly. Leslie and Vivie, both of whom normally accused me of being more lenient toward Jimmy because he was the baby of the family, began to lobby for his release from such severe punishment.

We were three weeks into the situation, when one afternoon Jimmy went over to his friend Bobby's house. It wasn't long before the phone rang. It was Jimmy, and he had a dilemma, he said. Bobby wanted to watch TV, and Jimmy wanted to stay with him. What should he do? I paused, allegedly to think over the situation, but in reality to control my mirth. I told him he could stay and watch TV with Bobby. That evening I declared that because of his honesty, the punishment was lifted. Even then I suspected that he was playing on my feelings. He knew me only too well and was, in reality, not only lifting the punishment imposed on him, but also giving me an honorable out. Years later he confirmed my suspicion. And many years later still, I stunned and amused Jimmy by revealing to him the true identity of the "reliable source." Kids are often on to the games we play, and if one is lucky, as we have been, we give each other room for saving face.

One day I found an open letter on Vivie and Leslie's desk, obviously left there for me to see. Addressed to Ann Landers and beginning, "We are two daughters of a mean mother," it recounted my unwillingness to let them participate in something of which I did not approve. When they came home from school, I asked them whether they needed a stamp. To the best of my knowledge, the letter was never mailed. We have had a lot of fun over the years when Vivie and Leslie have informed me that their daughters have had similar frustrations and accused them of unfairness. They're mildly annoyed that they have become "just like Mom."

Looking back now on my own and my children's early years, and on certain similarities of emotion and approach, I am awed that the two generations have held on to feelings that mirror each other, despite the enormous changes that have taken place in the world. I still remember vividly as a little girl walking with my maternal grandmother on a starlit night. When I mentioned how bright and large the moon seemed, Grandmother told me that the heavenly bodies are really much larger than they appear. When I inquired as to how large they were, her black-and-white shawl slid down her shoulders as she made a large circle with her arms, telling me earnestly that they were at least "THAT large." I am quite sure it was not an adjustment to a child's view, but that given her perspective on the world and science that she may truly have believed it. That was my grandmother. And now my granddaughter Jennifer talks about making a career at NASA in the space program.

Nonetheless, no matter how far apart our concepts of the universe, some things remain the same over the generations. When I think back now and steep myself in memories, I realize, on a purely intellectual level, that our children are grown and have children of their own. Yet, as parents we have not changed. Our children may lead busy, active lives that take them all over the world, but whenever they visit us or we visit them, Kurt and I sheepishly have to confess that, no matter how late the hour, we can't go to sleep until we once again hear the sounds that indicate that they have returned home safely.

The Sultan's Horse

MID-1960s AND REFLECTIONS ON 1946

I HAD OFTEN WONDERED how the sight of Paris would affect me after so many years. Would I see it as a tourist, recalling only dimly the sights I had seen years before? Or would familiar sights transport me back to the reality of days long past and evoke anew memories of events and situations I had since come to grips with? Which Paris would it be for me? The romantic city of my wedding day, with the scent of lilies of the valley, or the rain washed, mournful Paris I last saw through the windows of the hearse as I accompanied my uncle Leopold on his final journey?

Strangely it turned out to be neither. As I drove and walked through Paris again, along the Seine edged by stone embankments; along the quays past the bookstalls near Île de la Cité; along the boulevards, the Place de la République, the Place Saint-Michel, it all became as familiar as Main Street or the Safeway at home. And there, in the familiarity of Paris, one image persisted. It was not the memory of Kurt's and my wedding day, for the romantic love of that time had mellowed, deepening into the permanency of security and contentment of our everyday life together. Neither was it the memory of my uncle during the two visits I had paid him shortly after he had moved there from Turkey—not the first, when he surrounded me with Oriental splendor; nor the last, when we parted forever. I have since learned to dull the raw edges of pain, accepting loss, as we all must, in the course of living. But as I walked around Paris, seeing the old limestone buildings mellowed to a soft, soothing gray; hearing the cobblestones echo my footsteps at dusk; seeing the majesty of Notre Dame mirrored in the Seine, my memories turned nostalgic and filled with regrets. For me Paris is and will forever be closely linked with the memory of Monsieur Louis. And I will regret, as one must, the times when I neglected my duty. After my uncle Leo's divorce from Monsieur Louis's daughter, there came, of course, a break between our two families. Although I am sure my uncle retained a lot of respect and even affection for Monsieur Louis, I had to choose sides, and loyalty naturally made me choose my uncle.

Years passed. I was busy raising a family, occupied by the multitude of little details that provide such eloquent excuses for not fulfilling one's obligations. More years passed. Though the family quarrel was almost forgotten, every so often a peculiar uneasiness would well up in me, usually at the most unexpected moments. It would hit me while wheeling a baby carriage, setting the table for dinner, or closing a window against the rain. But I would squelch it quickly and return with renewed vigor to my task. Seeing Paris again, however, I could no longer turn my back on that gnawing guilt that had followed me through the years. It was futile to reason with myself that I actually owed Monsieur Louis nothing. He had been employed by my uncle all those years ago, and it had been to his benefit to help me. Nonetheless I knew better. Every corner of Paris brought back a poignant memory of him, a sage who knew the art of living and who had opened the gates of adult life for me, affording me a glimpse of what lay ahead. And, tempering his lessons with compassion for the impetuousness of my youth, he had cloaked his knowledge in an antiquated eccentricity I always remembered (although I had ridiculed it at the time). Thus he had given me priceless advice, for he was the first person to teach me that nothing is ever completely perfect: "In order to enjoy the pleasures that life offers," he said, "one must never wait for the perfect day, but make the day perfect with whatever little joy might come along."

In his wisdom, I am sure, he understood even my silence and did not blame me for it. It was in Paris, where the memory of him stirred me so deeply, that I finally faced myself and realized I had been wrong. I would give a great deal if I could write to him today, saying, "The differences between your family and mine have nothing to do with my feelings for you. I think of you often, fondly, and with gratitude." In twenty-five words I could have cleansed my conscience through this simple statement of a truth that would have hurt no one. But the truth is often realized too late. For Monsieur Louis died last year, and it does not matter to him or anyone else now. It matters only to me.

Yet somehow I don't feel sad. I know that when I stroll the boulevards, see the chestnut trees in bloom, taste the golden wine, enjoy the *bon café*, and smell the fragrance of violets on a flower cart after the rain, I am paying tribute to him. When I see Paris as he showed it to me—at dusk on a spring evening from an old hansom cab—when I feel with my senses what is offered to me for no matter how fleeting a moment, then I pay tribute to his memory—the consummate bon vivant.

THE COACHMAN SAT PERCHED ON HIS SEAT, idly playing with the reins; the horse's back gleamed in the fading sunlight. The statue of Napoleon as Caesar was still fully bathed in the golden rays of the setting sun while the cobblestone square was already being invaded by oblique shadows. The Place Vendôme seemed to have remained unchanged through the centuries. The mellow softness of the surrounding buildings, touched now by the fleeting gold of the sun, seemed grateful for the shroud of darkness. It was certainly a well-deserved rest at their venerable age. Their solidness was comforting, for one had the feeling that the pattern of life would remain unchanged for those within their walls.

The horse and the man who held the reins seemed part of the unchanging picture. The coachman greeted us, "Monsieur, 'dame." His hand went up to his hat and swept into a gesture indicating the threadbare, mustard-colored seat. I was ready to enter, but Monsieur Louis's hand detained me.

"*Combien, Monsieur?*" he asked. The coachman named the price. "What?" Mr. Louis's arms went up in horror. "You must have misunderstood me, *mon cher ami*. I said a ride through the Jardins des Tuileries, not to Marseilles."

"*Oui, Monsieur,*" the coachman asserted. "I understood you perfectly, but that is the price."

I felt myself blushing over the indignity of the haggling and tried to tell Monsieur Louis that I really didn't care if we took the ride or not.

My thoughts were thousands of miles away with my fiancé, Kurt, in the United States. Thanks to endless paperwork obstacles, our reunion was uncertain, and I despaired of our ever being together again. My desire to emigrate to America was all I could think about. But Monsieur Louis seemed not to have heard me; he was completely engrossed in the conversation.

The coachman, a trifle annoyed, was saying lazily, "Why don't you hire a taxi, Monsieur? It is cheaper and faster."

Monsieur Louis's hands came to rest on his hips. He let the coachman finish. A moment's silence hung between them. I wondered if Monsieur Louis was at a loss for words. The coachman looked at him, too. Then he spoke.

"A *taxi*?" making it sound like "an *ambulance*?" "*Cher ami*, what are you suggesting? What pleasure would there be in a taxi ride on a spring evening?" Unfailingly he had appealed to the loyal heart of old Paris. Pride gleamed in the coachman's eyes.

"Ah, *certainement*," the coachman answered. "It is the fragrance of Paris, the bouquet . . ."

"And to know it is to love it." Monsieur Louis's eyes looked into the dusk as if looking back on a memory. There was a moment's silence in the understanding of two loyal hearts. But Monsieur Louis had met his equal. For, shrewdly, the old coachman ever so gently picked up the thread of their understanding and wove on.

"Ah," he said, cocking his gray eyebrows. "Those pleasures are rare; they have become very rare in this fast age. To enjoy that pleasure, to recapture a memory, one must be prepared to pay a price." The last word stood alone, as the scent of the word *pleasure* drifted into the spring air of the Place Vendôme and mingled with its fragrance, and the word *price* landed neatly at Monsieur Louis's feet. A volatile smile passed over his inscrutable face.

"Then that's the price," he said soberly.

"That's the price," the coachman repeated.

"*Bon.*" Monsieur Louis started to walk away, but turned as if a fresh thought had just occurred to him. "Then how about selling me that horse?" he asked.

"*Avec plaisir, Monsieur, avec plaisir.*" The coachman struggled out of his seat and handed Monsieur Louis the reins, naming a price.

"The price isn't bad," Monsieur Louis mused. "Not bad at all. The horse isn't bad, not bad at all." Monsieur Louis patted the horse's flank, touched its nose, stroked the hide upward, and pulled the animal's lips apart. It bared an awful grin. "Hmmm," Monsieur Louis remarked. "How old is the horse?"

"Eleven years," the owner answered.

"On which side was it?" Monsieur Louis asked matter-of-factly. Then, without waiting for a reply, he centered his entire attention on the animal's left leg. "When was it broken?" he asked. Again without waiting for an answer, he continued. "Didn't set too well; you should have it looked after."

"You know a lot about horses, Monsieur," the coachman said in anxious admiration. "Are you English? Do you have stables?"

"No." Monsieur Louis's voice was heavy with regret. "I was a ship's captain in the Dardanelles, mostly rough waters, treacherous waters. On bad days, on stormy days out at sea, you know what I thought? I thought that when I got old I would like to get a horse and ride around Paris."

"Buy it then, Monsieur," the coachman urged without conviction. Their game was over; the fun had gone out of the bartering, and the coachman bent over the horse's broken leg, recognizing the faltering source of income. With his uncanny sense of timing and the precision he must have used when navigating turbulent waters, Monsieur Louis seized the moment and held it. Wearily he put his well-tended hands on the shiny lapels of the coachman's worn serge coat.

"I am *un homme des affaires*—a businessman," he said, again with obvious regret. "What would I do with a horse? But more important, far more important, *cher ami*, what would *you* do without him?"

"Ça va." The bargain was struck; they split the difference. The old springs groaned under our weight, and instantly the horse started to trot.

The coachman's back was perfectly straight; he sat on his perch with pride. After all, he was driving around Paris a man who appreciated all its charms. Dusk was falling across the Place Vendôme as the horse turned to pass the old Hotel Calais.

"This is a pleasant job you have," Monsieur Louis continued, "Other people have to pay for that pleasure."

"Oui," the man replied. "It is nice, but there is little money in it. It costs a lot to maintain a horse. I gave him shots the other day; you wouldn't believe how much those shots cost. And my wife, her shots cost almost as much as the horse's, and she's been sick for four years."

"What's wrong?" Monsieur Louis's voice was sincere with concern.

"She coughs all the time. That's all, coughs."

"Coughs? What does the doctor say?"

"Ah, Monsieur, those *docteurs*! They don't know. Wouldn't you think they could cure a simple cough? *Ah, non.* The place where we live is damp; it gets worse in the fall. They give her medicine, but she coughs and coughs. Wouldn't you think they could cure a woman's cough in four years? Non?" With that question he turned around to us. A taxi swerved; the driver honked, leaned out, shook his fists, and swore.

"A simple cough, for four years." The horse trotted on as if nodding his head in unison with his master's recitation of his problems.

"I would like to tell you something," Monsieur Louis said. "It never hurts to try, but in our family, we have a ridiculously simple method of curing a cough. It has often proved better than any medication."

"Oh, Monsieur," the coachman exclaimed, "Claudette will try any-thing, *anything!*"

"*Bon,* this is what you do. Do you know a farmer? Well, take your wife to the farm and get an egg from a hen while it is still warm. Break it into a dish that has been warmed in the oven. Take a piece of butter as large as the yolk, and two spoonfuls of sugar. Beat it fast, and have her eat it immediately. It sticks, you know—lubricates the throat."

"*C'est formidable!*" the coachman muttered, shaking his head and re-peating the remedy. "Thank you, Monsieur; if it helps poor Claudette, we will bless you."

"My mother got that recipe," Monsieur Louis concluded, "you will never guess where." He did not wait for a response. The coachman only shook his head.

"My mother was friendly with the ladies in a sultan's harem. One lady told her about it. They had lots of trouble with coughs and colds. And those marble floors get cold, especially at night. And some of the garments are very thin; you'd be surprised."

95

"Monsieur." The coachman pulled to the curb and stopped. "Monsieur," he was begging. "There are some questions I have always wanted to ask. You might be able to tell me. I might never have the chance again. Is it true, Monsieur—" Here he leaned over and whispered into Monsieur Louis's ear.

"Certainly!" Monsieur Louis exclaimed with laughter.

"Monsieur . . ." The coachman started tentatively, then halted and sent me a reproachful glance for my presence.

Monsieur Louis saw the anxiety in the man's eyes. He seemed vastly amused. "*Elle est jeune,*" he said, on an apologetic note.

I might be young, I thought indignantly, but I had more sense than to be telling foolish stories when there were such important things as my entire future to settle!

Monsieur Louis eased himself out of the seat and climbed on to the coachman's perch. I got a glimpse of his fine Italian hand-sewn shoes, his English suit, and his impeccable shirt. There he rode, high up, through Paris. When ladies looked up, he swept off his hat in greeting. I could not hear their conversation, only an occasional exclamation from the enlightened coachman as I sat frustrated and angry, alone in the backseat of the cab.

It was quite dark when the horse stopped outside a brightly lit restaurant. Monsieur Louis took out some bills to pay the fare.

"Oh, no," the coachman protested. "I could not take money from a friend."

"Business is business," came Monsieur Louis's reply as he started counting off the bills. When he came to the amount they had agreed on, he stopped. Was there a stiffening in the coachman's hand? But Monsieur Louis did not remove another bill. No tip? I wondered. Monsieur Louis reached into his breast pocket and removed a fine cigar.

"No tips among friends," he said. "Only gifts are permissible." The coachman put the cigar in his breast pocket, caressing the fine wrapping and patting the pocket twice.

"Good-bye, Monsieur," he said. And then, "Monsieur?"

"Yes?" asked Monsieur Louis?

"Are you *sure* you are not French?"

MONSIEUR LOUIS HAD THE ABILITY to impart to those who served him the notion that it was the highest privilege to do so, and he called everybody *cher ami.*

He ordered dinner with great care, pondering the wine list as a general would consult a map before a battle. Finally an agreement was reached. A bottle appeared, coated with the finest film of dust. The label, but only the label, was wiped clean. Mr. Louis put on his gold rimmed glasses and scrutinized it carefully, rubbing a finger ever so slightly over the somewhat wrinkled paper. The eyeglasses were tilted up. The cork was drawn, a bit of golden liquid poured into his glass. The waiter stood back. The glass was lifted to the light, passing under Monsieur Louis's nose. He sniffed the aroma lightly and sipped with the expertise of the connoisseur he was. A moment passed, then he nodded in agreement. My glass was filled. We were launched.

The first course appeared. It was trout, broiled to perfection. But I had no mind to eat, toying with my fork and thinking what my chances were of getting to America.

Sensing my restlessness and lack of appetite, Monsieur Louis pushed his own fish aside and waved away the waiter, who had appeared to inquire solicitously if everything was satisfactory.

He leaned toward me and asked, "How did you like the Tuileries?" I was caught off guard.

"Oh, very nice, very beautiful, really."

Monsieur Louis regarded me with his wise eyes, which never seemed to sleep. "It is a pity," he said, "that you didn't even see them. I thought, that by leaving you alone in the back of the coach you would have a good chance to observe it all. A pity, my child. Such memories are to be treasured. To be so young, to see Paris on a spring evening for the first time from a horse-drawn cab."

I felt ashamed, but before I could reply, he continued, "You will be a credit to your new country, my dear. You are very American, you know." I smiled at the undeserved compliment. "America is a new country," he said. "A young country. You are young, too, eager, impulsive, single-minded, and above all, impatient. Hurry, hurry, and accomplish more. Ah, yes, accomplish more. But how do you know how much you have accomplished already if you never have time to stop and look back?"

"Now, then," he said, and once again put on his glasses with care. He removed a gold pen from his pocket, took an empty cigarette box, opened its seams, and turned it over. He wrote: *Number 1. You want to go to America.* "Right?" He glanced over the glasses for my eager approval. *Number 2. You and Kurt want to get married.* "Those are our objectives. The problems? You can't get out of France or any other place, for that matter, because you have no papers. I have good news for you. Your uncle Leopold has a copy of your birth certificate, which your father sent, along with other papers, shortly before the beginning of the war. Although this may be of great help for proving your identity, it will not help you get to America because of the quota system. According to the quota, I understand, it might take five to six years. And that, of course, is an eternity when one is twenty-one."

How did he know? I wondered. "How about priority?" I asked. "I understood there was such a thing."

"Yes," he admitted, "but, according to the Americans, there are thousands of priority cases waiting. Now that the war is over, there is still a tremendous lack of shipping."

I looked at him, my eyes filling with tears at the thought of the injustice I had done him thinking that he did not take my plight seriously. At the same time, I felt a dawning realization of the hopelessness of my situation.

"Tell me, my dear," Monsieur Louis's voice changed suddenly. "You know, a thought just occurred to me a while ago during the ride, to be exact. I wonder if you have ever considered this: Some people never give themselves the joy of buying a painting that catches their fancy. I mean, they feel they have to have a home first, then a table, a chair, and so on. Perhaps *then* they buy a painting, and it's usually something that fits their home or whatever is fashionable at the moment, not perhaps really what they like."

Here was the same thing again, when I had hoped we could find some solution to the problem that had become the core of my existence. For a time we had seemed to have the situation so well in hand. Now we were off on a tangent again.

"What I mean, my dear, is, I wonder if you have any such notions."

"What notions?" I made an effort to be obliging.

"Do you care if you buy a table first or a painting?"

"I couldn't care less," I assured him. At that moment nothing seemed of importance but getting out of France.

He smiled. "Good," he said. "Good. I was afraid you might have some objections."

Why all this talk? I thought wildly. Suddenly one of his shrewd grins came over his face.

"Look," he said, pointing to number 1, which said, *You want to go to America,* under which he wrote, *table;* under number 2, which said, *You and Kurt want to get married,* he wrote, *painting.*

"Then you have no objection if we change the sequence?" he inquired with mock gravity. Somewhere within me recognition dawned.

"You mean . . . you mean?" I was almost stuttering.

"I mean," he said, "why not get married first and *then* go to America? Might save a honeymoon, too! As an American, your young man can travel. And once you are his wife, you will have no quota to overcome. Might also give the family an opportunity to meet him."

"Oh, Monsieur Louis!" I jumped up to embrace him, bursting with joy. How wonderful! How simply wonderful!

Miraculously the fish reappeared, sizzling hot again. The waiter had removed it when he saw it growing cold. I was speechless with happiness at the thought of how soon I might be seeing Kurt again, how wonderful everything would be. I could not eat.

After regarding me with benevolent silence for a moment, Monsieur Louis said, "First, you can't eat because you are *so* unhappy, and now you are *too* happy to eat—what a waste of emotion and of excellent trout! I hate to spoil your happiness with a dire prediction, but, my child, you must know that it may not be as simple as it appears. We might encounter obstacles we don't know about yet. The situation was not so hopeless before as it seemed, nor is the path as smooth now as you might believe. The answer is usually found somewhere in the middle. But," he said mockingly, "if we had not taken the ride, it might have never occurred to me."

Suddenly I was afraid again. Was I never to find simple solutions?

"Monsieur Louis," I asked with apprehension, "what if the authorities don't register me? What if he can't come? What if?"

He stopped me. "You are asking questions that people have asked since the beginning of time: 'What if?' My dear, I shall tell you something about the uselessness of 'what if.'" He then launched into a story that has given me amused sustenance during many a crisis.

Monsieur Louis's voice was deep; the words flowed slowly; he was a superb raconteur. *Many years ago there was a sultan who was mighty and wealthy. He had everything he could wish for—land stretching endlessly, palaces, wives, jewels.*

Monsieur Louis's voice made me see the vast expanse of the windswept desert, the slender white marble columns of the fabulous palaces, the graceful women in gold embroidered harem pants, the exotic flowers and music. Ships loaded with rubies, sapphires, spices. He had the ability to bring the splendor of the Arabian nights to the corner table of a Paris restaurant.

And there was the sultan, master of it all, sad because one ardent wish and desire remained unfulfilled in his life. Above everything he possessed, he loved his horse, a noble, pure white stallion. He would talk to this horse as a man would to a friend, and it seemed that the animal understood each word. Still it grieved the sultan no end that the animal, so intelligent, so devoted, so beautiful, could not talk.

Somewhere on earth, he thought, there must be someone who could teach the stallion to speak. He sent forth couriers through his lands and the lands across the sea in order to find a teacher for his beloved horse. But to no avail. One day as the sultan sat dejected and disappointed in his palace, the great vizier appeared before him. "Your Majesty," he said, "there is a man at the gate, a water carrier named Ahmed, who claims he can teach your horse to speak."

"Show him in immediately, show him in."

"But Your Majesty, this is a poor, insignificant-looking man."

"Show him in immediately!" the sultan commanded.

Monsieur Louis's voice changed with whomever he portrayed. The sultan's voice was melodious yet authoritative. The vizier's was harsh; his words cut like a knife. Monsieur Louis painted incredible word-pictures. I could almost see the slight, nervous man entering the sultan's chamber with a weasel-like gait, his small eyes darting, blinded by the magnificence of the chamber. I could see him fall to his knees in front of the sultan.

Surprisingly well spoken, he affirmed that he had been in close contact with horses since his childhood, when his own father worked as a cleaner of the royal stables. "I talked to horses, and they talked to me. I love horses more than humans," said the man.

"Did anyone witness the exchanges?" asked the sultan.

"No," replied the man with embarrassment. The vizier cut him short, but the mighty sultan seemed to listen.

"How long would it take to teach my stallion to talk?" asked the sultan.

"Well, it takes a child four or five years to learn to carry on a proper conversation. And even such a child would not be fit to converse with you, Mighty Sultan," said Ahmed.

Monsieur Louis paused to let me absorb the story

Ahmed continued, "The stallion must be superior, since he is so loved and adored by you, Mighty Sultan. Give me seven years, and I shall teach your horse to talk." The sultan agreed, the water carrier was named the teacher of the sultan's beloved horse, and the stables were converted into a schoolroom. Accommodations for the teacher and his family were in the royal palace.

Monsieur Louis took a long sip of his wine. I tried to listen, but my thoughts were too far away.

Time passed, and the teacher reported slow but steady progress. It seemed that the stallion needed more rest between the language lessons. Then one afternoon the stallion's teacher mounted his horse and rode into town to the bazaar.

Suddenly the bazaar was right in the restaurant with us. I could almost feel the oppressive heat of the afternoon, and hear the merchants hawking their wares, the flies buzzing around in endless numbers.

The teacher of the sultan's horse, riding a fine horse of his own, was greeted with the respect afforded a person of means. One of Ahmed's old water-carrier friends, burdened with heavy pails on his arms, approached. He set down his pails, and Ahmed dismounted, returning his old colleague's greeting. In conspiratorial intimacy, the friend asked the one question that had been on everyone's minds, almost the only topic of conversation at the bazaar. "Ahmed," he said, "Everyone knows that animals cannot talk. How

*are you getting away with living in splendor while promising to teach the
horse to speak?'*

*With scholarly words Ahmed enlightened his friend. "The horse is a su-
perior one," he said. "Why else would the sultan love him so much? He is
making steady progress, and seven years is a very long time. In seven years,
I might die or, heaven forbid, the sultan might die, or possibly the horse
might die. Or perhaps—the horse may learn to talk."*

Monsieur Louis put down his wine and looked at me with his wise
old eyes. He looked at me for a long time without blinking and said
softly, "So much for the 'what ifs.'" Still holding my eyes with his, he
called, "*Garçon. L'addition, s'il vous plaît!*" And very slowly, still looking
at me, he signed the bill.

Grandfather

*H*AVING BEEN LESS THAN A YEAR OLD WHEN HE DIED, I did not know my paternal grandfather. Yet he has had more influence on my thoughts—particularly about religion—than anyone else. I have two photographs of him. In both he is a very old man with a long white beard. His eyes are kind, wise, and somehow sad. Even the very existence of these photographs says a lot about the person he was. Toward the end of Grandfather's life, my father asked to have these pictures taken. Grandfather, a devoutly religious man, at first declined out of respect for the practice among many religious Jews that one should not make an image of a person. But my father pointed out that one day Grandfather's young—or as yet unborn—grandchildren would want to know what he looked like. Grandfather thought about the point and, open-minded even into his old age, consented to have what most likely were the only two photographs ever taken of him. Often I have tried to picture what God looks like, but always this photographic image of my aged, bearded grandfather comes into my mind's eye.

MY VISION OF MY GRANDFATHER is mostly seen through the prism of family trips to his hometown, Czortkow, to visit my grandmother, years after he had passed away. The town was near the Polish border with Russia and Romania, 710 kilometers from where I was born and grew up. It was just about as far as you could go and still be inside Poland's borders, but it might as well have been the other side of the moon in many respects. To travel from my hometown of Bielsko to Czortkow took a full twenty-four hours by fast train, and required changing trains in the middle of the night. Extensive preparations were made for that monumental trip: Provisions of all sorts—thermoses with hot and cold drinks, pillows, blankets, headache pills, and prayers for a safe journey—were all de rigueur.

It was all worth it. I loved going to Czortkow to see my grandmother and my father's extended family. We went almost every summer. I recall the excitement of our arrival. My uncles and cousins usually met us at the train: Two horse-drawn carriages stood in readiness outside the small station with the broken door and the taped-up ticket window that bore the official emblem of Poland—the likeness of a white eagle on a blood red background.

After much hugging and kissing and commotion, the luggage was loaded onto a much less elegant equipage, which followed our caravan to Grandmother's home. Upon our arrival, my grandmother and my aunts would be waiting outside the house. Grandmother was a tiny woman with a face resembling a withered winter apple. My father, Papa, who towered above her, would lift her up and kiss her on both cheeks while she squealed with delight. Then my mother, Mama, would kiss her mother-in-law's work-worn hand, and my brother, Artur, and I would follow suit. Grandmother would give us a hearty hug and kiss in return and recite a prayer of thanksgiving for our safe arrival.

When I went to bed in the tiny, whitewashed, unadorned room, in the high, simple iron bed, I always felt a certain at-homeness. This was strange, actually, as I reflect on it now, because I always liked frills and colors.

My most exciting memories of Czortkow were of going with Grandmother to the market on Thursdays to buy the ingredients for the Sabbath dinner. I must have been nine or ten when I last went there, yet the memories remain fresh and vivid seventy years later. I can still smell the warm, pungent odor of horses, I can still see sunflowers so tall that they seemed to me to tower over the matchbox-houses along the road, and there were glistening, liquid silver fish lying in wooden tubs, next to butter in the shape of large flowers glittering on brook-washed leaves. I have a vivid picture of Grandmother lifting a screeching, flailing chicken and feeling for plumpness while its white feathers flew all over us. Grandmother would be garbed in a long brown cotton dress that reached her ankles and a not-quite-matching brown babushka on her head. She would dole out *zlotys* and *groszys* to farmers, and then hand me a sun-warmed plum. Mama would step gingerly behind Grandmother, trying hard to enjoy the outing and smiling politely under her large summer hat.

Paintings by Marc Chagall vividly bring back Czortkow to me. They should. After all, Czortkow was not so far from Chagall's birthplace of Vitebsk.

But Friday night was special. A calm, almost holy silence descended over the little hamlet. Grandmother and Mama would light the Sabbath candles, while a diaphanous veil rested on Mama's dark hair like a crown. In almost hushed expectant tones, we would sing the hymn for the entrance of the honored "Sabbath bride," while outside the crooked fences bowed in reverence to her majesty.

Saturday afternoon, following services in the synagogue, was somehow both solemn and festive at the same time. Papa would be dressed in his cutaway, with a stiff-collared shirt and dark tie. Artur would wear long pants and a tie. Grandmother wearing a long black silk dress, and Mama, too, wearing a black silk long-sleeved dress with a black hat are indelible images in my mind. I did not relish the outing at all, always feeling rather hot and uncomfortable in long white stockings, black patent leather shoes, white long-sleeved dress, and a huge white bow that would continually slip out of my hair. We would almost always pay a respectful call upon the revered Czortkow *rebbe* and his wife. They lived in a formal, huge home near the synagogue, conducting something akin to a court to which his followers flocked from all over Poland and a good part of Europe, because he was a much-respected scholar, writer, and spiritual leader. Our family's prideful connection to him was through my grandfather, who was not only a disciple of sorts, but also a relative of the great man.

Papa and Artur would leave us in the courtyard of the rabbi's home as they paid their respects, while Grandmother, Mama, and I went to a different wing, which housed the apartment of the rabbi's wife. As we entered the large sunny room, where many women sat on sofas and chairs, the *rebbetzin*, as she was called, would stand up and approach us. She was tall and slim, wore a white-haired wig, and was elegantly dressed in black. She embraced my grandmother and kissed her on the cheek. Mama kissed her on the hand, as did I, while making a curtsey. The visit was always short. I do not recall what the adults talked about, but in parting I would be given an orange, wrapped in tissue paper on which was printed "Jaffa." It had come all the way from Palestine, I was told, and I was almost too awed to eat this treasure.

NOW, FINALLY, CAME THE BEST PART OF THE VISIT: The rest of the day was spent with Papa—and often I had him all to myself. While Grandmother and Mama were busy preparing the large late-afternoon meal, and Artur and our cousin David were off playing soccer, Papa would inquire—knowing well that I was waiting impatiently for him to ask—if I wanted to take a walk with him. That was our special time. With my small hand in his large, warm one, we started toward the woods. "Papa, please tell me the story!"

"Again?" He looked down at me, knowing precisely which story I wanted to hear. "Very well," he would begin. "It was before you were born, during the war [World War I]. This part of Poland was Austria [I knew all that, but it was part of the story]. Your uncles and I were in the Austrian army. My parents and your aunt Anna were here at home. We had fierce battles. Czortkow fell into the hands of the Russians. My brothers and I were in the other part of Austria, in Bielsko, where I met Mama. We were cut off from our parents and could not communicate with them for maybe a year. They worried terribly, of course, over what might have happened to us during the battles.

"Your grandfather was a very pious man," he continued. "He went to synagogue every day. But above all else, he liked to recite his morning prayers while walking in the woods. He loved animals and knew the names of all the flowers and trees. So, one morning he was walking in the woods—"

"Papa, maybe in this very place?" I interrupted.

"Maybe. Suddenly, he heard a lot of twittering. A little bird had fallen out of its nest, and the mother bird was hovering over it, unable to get it back. Grandfather knew that if he touched the bird, the mother would reject it. He found a branch, which looked like a fork, and lifted the little bird into the nest.

"At this point a couple of drunken Russian soldiers appeared and said that he was a *spy* and that he was putting up telephone wires in the trees. Well, your grandfather had never seen a telephone in his life! They took him to court, and he was convicted and sentenced to be banished—for the rest of his life—to Siberia.

At this point, I would usually start to cry. Papa usually picked me up and held me and kissed me. "You wanted to hear the story?"

"Yes, yes, Papa," I replied.

"But you have heard it a hundred times from Grandmother and me. How she and Aunt Anna cried when they said good-bye to Grandfather. How he took only a small sack with a few clothes along with his sacred *tallith* and his tattered prayer book. They thought they would probably never see or hear from him again. They did not know whether my brothers or I were still alive. It was very, very difficult for them," Papa would say softly.

"It was a few years later," Papa continued. "The war was over, and Mama and I were married, and Artur was already born a year later, when I received this incredible telegram in Bielsko that Grandfather had returned! When I finally heard the whole story, I learned that one day he walked into his house, a thin old man with a very long gray beard. He kissed his family and his beloved books and, of course, Grandmother and Aunt Anna. And all my brothers, who now were living again in Czortkow, were excitedly talking in disbelief of their good fortune that Grandfather had returned. But Grandfather did not ask about me. Not seeing me in the house with the rest of the family, he assumed that I had been killed in the war, and he did not want to spoil the joy of his homecoming for them by mentioning me.

"Suddenly Grandmother jumped up, ran to her bedroom, and got Artur's baby pictures, handed them to Grandfather, and said, 'Look at your grandson—Julius's son!' When they explained, he broke down and started to cry. He talked about his ordeal. During his banishment in Siberia, he ate only vegetables, mostly turnips, and potatoes baked in the ashes of fires, perhaps some fruit when it was in season and available. He did not eat meat because it was not kosher. He talked about how, when the war ended, and 'political' prisoners were released, he had a very, very long journey home. It took more than a year, mostly on foot, sometimes on a peasant's wagon, working for farmers for a little food, never traveling on the Sabbath. It was a miracle that he survived and made it home safely."

Papa would then relate the rest of the story: how he and Mama made arrangements to get to Czortkow as quickly as they could. It was a big ordeal not only to see Grandfather, but this was also to be the first time that the rest of the family would actually meet Mama and Artur, who was still just a small baby. My maternal grandmother, whom we called *Omama*, wanting to impress her in-laws with her famed Viennese-style cuisine, cooked and baked all her specialties: Linzer torte, Dobos torte, and other delicacies. These, along with her famed chicken, were packed in boxes and baskets for the train ride to Czortkow. Mama's wardrobe was quickly refreshed; Artur was given his first suit—I remember seeing pictures of him as a baby in the velvet Fauntleroy suit trimmed with lace.

A superb raconteur, Papa would explain how nervous Mama was about the reception she would get from her new family. She was, of course, so beautiful, he told me, and she felt very self-conscious about being more worldly than her in-laws, and even foreign to them, in some ways. She did not speak Yiddish fluently, only German, and her upbringing had not been as religiously observant as Papa's.

Through Papa's words, I could visualize Mama, elegant in a dark blue dress and white hat, kissing Grandmother's and Grandfather's hands on her arrival in Czortkow. So, too, I could conjure up in my mind the picture of Papa, with Artur in his arms, embracing his father; and Grandfather, in turn, greeting Papa with the biblical words of Jacob greeting his lost son, Joseph: "I never thought I will see thy face again . . . and God showeth me the face of your son."

After the greetings were completed, Mama in her innocence started unpacking all the delicacies in her mother-in-law's strictly kosher kitchen. Obviously, Mama had a lapse of judgment in the entire matter of the food, and she placed some of her mother's succulent chicken on a plate and asked Grandfather to sample it. While the rest of the family looked on in speechless horror, Grandfather gazed at the daughter-in-law he had just met, and then at the chicken.

"That chicken looks very delicious, my dear daughter," Grandfather intoned. With that, he went to wash his hands, recited a short blessing, broke off a piece of the chicken, and ate it. Even as a young child who did not fully understand the significance of the story, it moved me. Here was my grandfather, who for years in the loneliness and deprivation of Siberia would not touch meat because it did not meet his rigid kosher standards, yet he would not insult his daughter-in-law's concept of kosher by deeming it to be less worthy than his own. With that story, and a few others, my grandfather, whom I never met, became my own lodestar in the bitterness, loneliness, and horror of the slave labor camps that I would endure as a young woman. If an old man could endure what he did, I reasoned, certainly I must, in his blessed memory, try to endure my own trials; and perhaps, like him, by some miracle I, too, would be reunited with my family.

As Papa and I would be nearing home and approaching the time-worn stone bench on which Grandmother would often sit, peeling potatoes or shelling peas, I would take Papa's hand and pull him toward it, imploring him with the familiar request for another beloved story. Papa would always comply, recounting the time, as a small boy, he sat next to his father on that bench on a Friday morning long ago. A wisp of a young girl in a tattered dress approached Grandfather and carefully held forth a little bowl. Shyly she whispered the question that her mother had asked her to pose to Grandfather: She wanted to know if the broken egg in the bowl was kosher. Grandfather took the bowl and slowly let the egg white wash over the yolk that was blemished by a blood spot. Now, everybody, even my father as a young boy, knew that such an egg was not kosher. But Grandfather thoughtfully and tenderly tilted the bowl this way and that. Finally he said, "Tell your mother that this egg is kosher and it will make a fine challah for tonight." He softly touched the girl's bangs and uttered a benediction.

When the girl had left, Papa was shocked. "Everybody knows that an egg with a blood drop in it is not kosher!" he insisted.

"Yes, my son, the girl's mother knows that the egg is not kosher, but it is probably the only egg she has," Grandfather replied.

"Then we should give her one," Papa answered.

"No, my child, this proud woman does not want charity. If a widow with four young children wants to extol God and honor the Sabbath by baking a challah, then I believe the egg is kosher in the eyes of God," said Grandfather, ending the conversation.

GRANDFATHER! HOW OFTEN IN MY LIFE'S JOURNEY have I have thought of him and been guided by his deeds. In the years after the war, I always wanted to think of him during the Jewish holidays while I was in synagogue. But somehow I could never connect with him in lofty structures adorned with grand pillars or stained-glass windows. But once, in 1963, I felt his spirit especially close to me. I was in Israel, in Safed, the mysterious kabalistic mountain enclave, with its many artisans and galleries. I wandered away from one gallery and saw a tiny courtyard. I approached it. At the far end opened an old heavy, wooden door. I stepped through the doorway and found myself in a tiny prayer room. Along the wall was a plain cupboard of unvarnished wood. I opened it, and inside stood a Torah. It wore no crown, no velvet, no gold-embroidered mantle—just a simple cover of homespun linen. Here stood the sacred symbol of my faith in completely unadorned majesty. I wanted to kiss it. But I knew that one must wash one's hands and cleanse one's heart before touching a sacred object. I knew, too, that as a woman, according to strictly Orthodox practices, I was not supposed to touch the Torah. But even at this, I rationalized that perhaps my grandfather's enlightened view of Judaism might make my next act not only permissible but appropriate. I reached into my purse and found a wrapped towelette that the airlines provide. I opened it, allowed the perfume aroma to fade a bit, and cleaned my hands. Then I reverently touched the symbol of my faith. I somehow felt very connected with my grandfather.

Author's grandfather

Meet My Son

O UR AMERICAN GROUP HUDDLED CLOSE TOGETHER, waiting to enter the dining room of the Marriott Hotel in Amsterdam. Though it had been more than twenty-four hours since we left New York, after only a brief interval to freshen up, we bravely banished the usual postarrival fatigue from our eyes and got ready for dinner with our hostesses—members of the Dutch Jewish community and other dignitaries.

A group of Dutchwomen approached us, spontaneously switching to English as they came near. There were introductions all around. A vivacious-looking woman in handsome tweeds flashed a warm smile.

"My name is Frieda Menco," she said, stretching out a strong hand.

When I told her mine, she embraced me, saying: "I know you from your book. We have much in common. I want to interview you. Will you do that? I am a writer."

Bewildered and pleased, I readily acquiesced.

The milling throng swept us up and separated us. I wound up at a different table, but after dinner we managed another brief conversation, in which she told me about her work, which included writing a newspaper column as well as doing a radio interview program.

She extended a gracious invitation to tea at her home the following afternoon.

The next day, punctually at 3 P.M., I hailed a taxi in front of my hotel. It was one of those small, boxy, colorful vehicles, looking—like everything else in Holland—efficient, clean, and somehow scaled down.

I no sooner showed the driver the address than he lapsed into English.

As the car spun into motion, he automatically began to point out sights of interest. It seemed I had unwittingly picked a superb guide. During the short ride, we drove across several picturesque bridges, under which boats glided with graceful ease.

We came to a halt at one point as a veritable fleet of bicycles crossed the street in front of us. Riders of every age, from blue-jeaned kids to distinguished looking white-haired ladies and gentlemen, pedaled sedately before us.

Yielding to an impulse, as I do on occasion, I tried to envision how certain people would look in traditional dress. I had started this game on the KLM flight when I first saw the flaxen-haired stewardesses in their smart airline uniforms, picturing them in the peaked, starched white bonnets of little Dutch girls. Instead of walking up the aisles of our plane, they could be strolling along country lanes, among fields of bright, blooming tulips and spinning windmills.

At the hotel I could imagine the doorman in the customary old-fashioned Dutch dress, smoking a clay pipe and wearing wooden shoes. His stocky build and ruddy complexion fitted such a picture to perfection.

So now I spun that fantasy with the bicyclists.

I remembered with amusement that some years ago I had encountered a man in Texas who seemed the epitome of the Lone Star cowboy: tall, rugged, taciturn, a man obviously at home in the saddle. When I mentioned my fantasy to my Texas hosts, they informed me with great mirth that he was really an accountant from Rochester, New York.

But there in Amsterdam, there was no one to dispel my reverie, and so I dreamed on as I passed the magnificent Rijksmuseum, of which I had heard so much. It houses an unsurpassed collection of Goyas, El Grecos, Van Dycks, and Rubenses, to name but a few. Probably the most valuable canvas in the world, Rembrandt's *The Night Watch*, can also be found there. I promised myself that I would take the time to see it.

We passed the Vincent van Gogh Museum, all very bright and modern; I resolved I had to see that, too, before my departure.

The driver deftly made his way to our destination, depositing me in front of a handsome house on a tree-shaded street just off a beautiful canal. I was fifteen minutes early, which gave me the impetus to walk a bit.

The street, as I had come to expect in Holland, was spotlessly clean, verifying what I had heard as a child: Dutch housewives wash not only the floors of their homes each day but the sidewalks as well.

There was a profusion of flowers everywhere and another delightful sight: The curtains—most of them white, almost all made of lace in a variety of patterns, stiffly starched—could be seen through spotless windowpanes or billowing through open windows. They were like fanciful paper doilies, framing a delicious confection inside.

Walking along, I encountered a young Dutch mother steering a high-wheeled baby carriage. We resorted to the universal language of smiles and nods, which needed no interpreter, as I admired her apple-cheeked infant, sleeping peacefully in a heavy yellow sweater.

A few minutes after three-thirty, I opened the waxed light wood door and ascended a very steep flight of stairs. At the top of the landing, I was confronted by a bank of bells, and when I rang the appropriate one, in short order I heard the voice of my hostess call out, "Coming! Welcome to my home!"

We ascended another steep flight of stairs; she motioned me through a sequence of doors, at the end of which I found myself in a cozy living room.

As we chatted easily of this and that, I was struck again at how well informed my hostess was on current events, how well acquainted with personalities in American political life, literature, and the arts. I felt I was no match when it came to European affairs.

HER LIVING ROOM WAS FILLED with beautiful, contemporary Scandinavian furniture. The atmosphere was intimate and homey. There was a profusion of flowers: apricot-colored roses, perhaps four dozen of them, reposing in an earthen bucket on the floor, others in chunky glass vases in delightful disarray. I could almost see my hostess approaching the flower vendor, saying breezily, "I'll take them all," then lugging them home and putting them down at random without even taking off her hat.

Marvelous modern art, smartly framed in chrome or pewter, graced the tall white walls. Sculpture, bold yet graceful, apparently chosen with the unerring eye of a connoisseur, adorned on tables and shelves. Green apples gleamed in a Delft bowl on the low table in front of us, on which rested a decanter with sherry and a teapot on an attractive tray, along with cheese and crackers.

I felt a sense of comfort and of *déjà vu*. Why? Suddenly it came to me. The open window with the breeze bringing the curtains in, the fragrance of the slightly chilly day, reminded me of so many similar days of my childhood in Poland. Were I now at home in Buffalo, I would have turned up the thermostat—something that was never available during my childhood years in Europe long ago—to drive the chill from the room. Instead, we would have put on sweaters and inhaled the bracing air, perfumed with roses and green apples.

"Time to work," my hostess informed me, as she led me to an adjacent room, furnished much like her living room, but virtually bursting with bookcases. We sat down at a plain, high worktable, on which were stacked mountains of paper and brochures.

She pushed forward an enormous tape recorder, adjusted a multitude of buttons, then rewound some tape to the usual garbled Donald Duck noises, just as a handsome young man entered the room. "Meet my son," she said.

He was twenty-one, spoke flawless English, and had just returned from a visit to the United States. We chatted amiably for a while.

Before the formal introduction of the program we were taping, I gleaned a bit of additional information about Frieda. She contributed regularly to the prestigious Dutch magazine called *Margriet*, writing provocative articles on marriage and family. She also conducted a weekly thirty-five-minute radio program for the Dutch Broadcasting Corporation, which was broadcast in Flemish to Belgium. When a special documentary was made on Auschwitz, she was entrusted with the task.

She had helped to found and run a successful management-consulting agency. The previous year she had been on a lecture tour of the United States, and she would be bound for London the following morning to begin a similar assignment.

When the recorder was finally switched off, my session finished, I felt I could turn the tables and ask her a few questions as well.

Frieda told me that her family could trace its ancestry in Holland for 350 years. Good friends had hidden them from the Nazis until September 1944, but they were betrayed and subsequently deported to Auschwitz with the last transport that left Holland.

In the recesses of my mind I remembered something. I ventured, "Wasn't that the transport on which Anne Frank and her family were deported?"

"Yes," she said quietly.

"Did you know her?" I pushed on.

"Yes," she replied again in the same even tone. "We were the same age. Our mothers knew each other well."

There was silence between us.

I WAS IN AMSTERDAM, THE CITY WHERE ANNE FRANK HAD LIVED. The immortal girl whose face would remain forever young, her large, dark eyes caught by the lens and arrested for posterity. Anne Frank, who had written her innermost thoughts just for herself in Amsterdam, and had become the chronicler of the great tragedy, her words conveying more of the climate of her times than most of the volumes compiled by all the historians on the Nazi era.

I was sitting in the comfortable, contemporary home of a well-informed, highly articulate Dutchwoman of approximately my age. She had known Anne Frank in Auschwitz. Was it an imposition to ask such questions? She was looking at me as if reading my thoughts. "I realize," I started, "that everyone quite likely asks you the same questions. Do you mind just a few more?"

She looked at me for a moment, her expressive eyes on me. I didn't flinch. "You know why I am asking," I said evenly. She nodded.

"Well, you can imagine what it was like in Auschwitz." Her voice trailed off. "I remember one time we were on a work detail together, carrying stones—huge, massive rocks . . .

"All our hair had been shaved off. Nonetheless she always managed to retain her spunk. Her older sister, Margot, was more withdrawn.

"Anne was a friendly girl, with delicate features, large eyes set in a very small, white face.

"Strangely, our mothers addressed each other formally as Mrs. Frank and Mrs. Brommet, even under those conditions. I guess that all they wanted was to survive with a semblance of dignity."

After a long pause for reflection, she picked up the story again.

"Anne was shipped to Bergen-Belsen, you know."

Yes, I knew that. "And you?" I continued.

"I stayed in Auschwitz."

As if to dispel my amazement, she added, "You know, when the Russian front was coming closer, and the Nazis had to abandon the camp in the winter of 1945, they set dynamite around the place in order to destroy the evidence. The inmates were left behind, for the machinery of death was no longer operational. Do you know what happened?"

I shook my head.

"When they set fire to the barracks, the wind blew in the opposite direction and we were spared. I was far too sick to be conscious of the events around me. We had no food for seven days, and I was delirious. I have only vague memories of a blood-red sky and seeing figures dressed in white coming into the barracks, carrying lighted candles.

"I was sure that I had died and was seeing angels, but they were Russian troops in winter uniforms, and they liberated us. Then a doctor from Bratislava brought me an egg. He saved my life."

Frieda returned to Holland after the war and did secretarial work once her strength returned. She speaks Greek, Latin, Dutch, English, German, and French and understands Italian and Spanish. She married in 1951, has two sons, and is now divorced. Physically she never fully recovered. She must rest frequently, for her muscles are damaged.

Mentally she is a giant, an intellectual stimulated by all forms of art. She particularly loves jazz because it makes her feel alive, cosmic, and vibrant.

Though we touched on many subjects of mutual interest, somehow the encounter had still another dimension. I realized that I was in the presence of an Anne Frank who *lived*. That it might have been a dark-eyed, middle-aged woman who had extended her hand to me in the dining room of the Marriott Hotel, who might have said, "My name is

Anne. I am a writer. Come, let us have tea together tomorrow afternoon at my house."

HER HOUSE. ANNE FRANK'S HOUSE.

My first visit to the Anne Frank House, at 263 Prinsengracht, on a narrow canal, took place in the evening. Three windows high and three windows wide, it was built in 1635, close to the canal, so that merchandise transported on the waterways could literally be brought to the doorstep. A houseboat was tied to a mooring in front of the structure, and I noticed that checkered gingham curtains, tied back with sashes, graced the windows.

A light inside framed the loaf of bread and bowl of apples on the table, so that it appeared to be a still life by a Dutch old master. It was so lonely and empty there. I thought of the young girls shut off from life so many years ago in that very house.

Something compelled me to see the house again in daylight, when its windows were mirrored in the canal like blind, unseeing eyes. The steps were as steep as the rungs of a ladder, the rooms smaller than I had imagined, yet so terribly empty that the void within wailed with an eerie voice.

I stepped gingerly, apprehensively, lest my footsteps betray my presence to an enemy below. I stroked the whitewashed wall, and I was overcome to see the black pencil marks by which the Franks and van Daans (that was the name Anne gave them; their real name was van Pels) had recorded the growth of their teenage children. At one point the marks had simply come to a stop. I looked at the small map dotted with pins with which Otto Frank had recorded the Allied advance through Normandy.

In the shared room in which Anne slept, there was pathetic evidence of the people she evidently admired: photographs of Deanna Durbin, of the young Ray Milland, of Ginger Rogers, and of the British princesses, Elizabeth and Margaret Rose. No furniture was left in the tiny chambers, just the small stove that was used to cook the food and burn the refuse, and the toilet, which could not be flushed by day lest the noise betray the occupants of the hideout.

I stood by the window, whose shades had to be drawn by day for all of those years of hiding, and I looked out at the quadrangle of the diminutive garden.

Sunflowers stretched skyward, and there in the shade of a tree now mightily grown—the same horse chestnut tree of which Anne had written—a pair of swings stirred gently in the breeze.

Those swings . . . whose children play on them? They could have been Anne's grandchildren by now.

Among the debris in this house a small book was found, to whose pages an adolescent girl had confided her innermost thoughts.

Traveling throughout the Netherlands, I saw the country through the eyes of Anne Frank. Eating dinner on a luxurious boat gliding along quiet canals, under bridges adorned with strings of lights, past ancient dwellings, illuminated as if in greeting. Heavy silver would grace the table, the food would be tastefully arranged, the wine chilled to the right degree, the ambience underscored by lilting music.

I thought of Anne.

Later in The Hague, where our group of American women was invited to tea at the home of the American ambassador, we strolled among beautiful gardens brilliant with flowers. Anne had written how she hungered for the touch of flowers, for the smell of freedom.

Would she have cheered her aging queen? Anne had written that Holland and not Germany was her home now. She might have felt a connection. As a young woman, Queen Juliana herself had endured the war in exile.

Anne, who so loved color and pageantry, probably would have come to The Hague on the third Tuesday in September to see the queen open parliament, resplendent in a golden coach drawn by eight magnificent horses.

I thought of how Anne would have brought her grandchildren to watch the procession, to picnic by the placid lake where fountains play and swans preen themselves beneath the willow trees.

I thought of her as I was seated in the ornate hall of Amsterdam's Koninklijk Instituut voor de Troopen (Royal Institute for the Troops).

The air was filled with anticipation; every seat was taken, and the gallery was filled to overflowing. Television cameras stood poised. The first few rows were reserved for the honorees, all elderly, all gray haired. A single violin was playing.

The lord mayor of Amsterdam, wearing his chain of office, stepped to the dais. Mrs. E. A. Haars, state secretary of justice, spoke. Then came the presentation by S. Argov, Israel's ambassador to the Netherlands.

> *Once again we come together to pay homage to a group of decent Dutchmen and -women who not so very long ago dared, at great peril to themselves and their families, to cling to their humanity and decency while the world around them was sinking into un-precedented barbarism. Once again we are assembled in order to express to them and to all those others represented by them, the gratitude and admiration of the Jewish people for saving the lives of desperate men, women, and children.*

Medals were placed around the necks of the old men and women as applause turned into a standing ovation and the clapping went on and on. Then, in the reception line, we met the heroes: the bakers and the seamstresses and the farmers. Pride glowing in their eyes, they showed pictures of those they had saved—their children, as they referred to them, who now have children of their own.

I thought of Anne, for she was right when she wrote, ". . . I still believe, in spite of everything, that people are truly good at heart."

I thought of her in the concert halls and libraries, and wondered what achievements would have been hers had she lived.

But I grieved for her not for the fame, the recognition, and the wealth that might have been hers, but for the simple human right to live and to enjoy life. To see a sunny day, a starry night. To sit in the home of a new friend while white curtains billowed in the breeze and the scent of fresh roses filled the air. To reminisce with a friend who knew her in Auschwitz when they both were young girls and lugged stones and still dreamed dreams. What I grieved for most was that she had been denied the joy of ever saying the words, "Meet my son."

Flight

LATE 1970s, CHICAGO, ILLINOIS

THE WOMAN APPROACHED ME. "You are . . .?" she said haltingly, and I nodded. She bore a striking resemblance to her mother, whom I remembered as an elderly woman and who when I last saw her, must have been a good fifteen years younger than the daughter who stood before me now. Tears were streaming down our faces; there were so many pent-up feelings waiting to be expressed, but neither of us could articulate them.

Standing at the overseas airline counter, I watched her check in her luggage. Behind the agent, a sign said WARSAW—FLIGHT X256. Was there actually a Warsaw? Was there still a Bielsko, our hometown, where we had last seen each other almost forty years ago? I no longer recalled that meeting, but it had likely taken place on a June day such as this, at the end of the last elementary school year, after which we would be attending different schools. Had anyone predicted then that our next encounter would be four decades later at one of the world's largest airports, we would have dismissed the thought as sheer fantasy.

The interval since then had seen the total destruction of our world; everything we loved and had been a part of was gone. Now she was on her way to visit the remains of a world that was no more, and I was awed by her decision. I could imagine such a trip only with a great deal of trepidation.

How strange this meeting was turning out to be. I found myself speaking to Lucy about mundane trivia, my mind and emotions racing ahead of the words, operating on two distinct levels, desperately searching for some clues of the past, some common ground that would tie us to the present. She produced a school picture, and, to my surprise, I was able to reel off name after name, something I would have regarded as an impossible feat only minutes earlier. Picking out Lucy on that picture seemed to superimpose the two images as in a viewfinder, blurred at first, then more sharply focused. There was the twelve-year-old, with what I knew to be heavy reddish braids falling over her shoulders, looking straight at the camera, clearly suppressing a smile that nevertheless turned up the corners of her mouth. It was precisely that unique smile I remembered now, its vestiges still etched on her aging face.

"This dress—" she said, pointing to her image on the photo, and I finished the sentence, "—it was green velvet." I could palpably recall the atmosphere of the schoolyard where we had posed, the scent of apple blossoms in the air. Our talk became a wild mélange of the past, fused with an acceptance of the present. Heretofore forgotten names, incidents, anecdotes spilled forth, leaving us breathless in trying to evoke those images. They had been relegated to a never-never land all those years, not seeming to ever have had any reality. Yet, here they were, incontrovertible proof that they had indeed existed.

Inevitably, she inquired about my parents, my brother. I shook my head. Instead I talked about my husband, my children, and my new grandchildren. Strolling about the long ramps at O'Hare, avoiding near collisions with scurrying strangers, peripherally taking in the constant flow of flight information that came over the PA system, we randomly spilled out details of our present lives until she said, "My father . . . I know what happened to my father. I know where and how he died. He was in Sosnowitz, you know, where they made him clean the streets of horse manure—our former cleaning woman wrote me about it. How she would leave small food packages along his route, hiding them in places she was able to inform him about."

A man, carrying two beige suitcases, came toward us, separating us for a moment. "Sorry," he said with a sheepish smile, and I noticed that his lightweight suit jacket was open, the stripes of his tie an exact match to the stripes on his shirt.

Lucy continued her stream of words, as I tried to summon up the image of her father in my mind. Somehow it had become vague and elusive. Although we were speaking English, the timbre of Lucy's voice brought back an afternoon in her home. We had managed to get hold of a stack of *True Romance* magazines that belonged to her older sister and were furtively devouring their "forbidden" contents. So engrossed were we in them that we nearly didn't notice the sound of a key turning in the front door. But the clomp of approaching footsteps galvanized us into action, and we desperately scurried to hide the "scandalous" literature.

I recalled now how Lucy's parents had entered the room. Her mother was short, slender, and red-haired. Suddenly now her father's pale profile leaped into my consciousness, as he had looked then. Lucy underscored what was in my mind. "At the *Aussiedlung*, the dreaded 'resettlement', they told him to get on the truck," she was saying. "For some reason he refused . . . they shot him . . . he fell dead in the street." A young girl, carrying a Coke from a vending machine, ran across our path. That stopped us for a moment. "I'm glad to know how he died," she went on. "He didn't suffer long." The irony ran through my mind, how fearful I had been that afternoon that he would find out about our clandestine pleasures and how all his own hopes and fears had come to nothing.

The initial formalities for an overseas flight completed, we felt the need to get out of the terminal building. We crossed the arterial network that rings O'Hare and made our way to a hotel coffee shop. Its futuristic decor rendered our reunion even more bizarre. After we had placed an order, Lucy filled me in about her brother. I remembered that he was her junior by several years, and we had always referred to him as "Little Paul." Lucy had witnessed the end of the war in Czechoslovakia, as had I, after surviving a succession of slave labor and concentration camps. Although our experiences had been similar, our paths had never crossed during the entire period. After liberation she, along with some friends her age, had found refuge with a Czech family. Subsequently, two of those girls had decided to move on to Munich, which had become one of the great centers for "displaced persons," the euphemism for all of us who had survived Hitler's inferno.

During those difficult days, the need to obtain news of your family, either directly or indirectly, was an ever-present specter, a constant struggle between hope and fear. It turned into an obsessive—and for most of us utterly futile—search across the length and breadth of the European continent, but one in which all survivors were continually engaged.

Now Lucy was relating to me how the Czech woman who had taken her into her home had called up to her room one evening, letting her know that a soldier had come to talk to her. "A soldier?" she queried, incredulously. "What does he want?" Lucy slowly went downstairs, her heart in her throat. In the hallway stood a tall young man in uniform.

He spoke in a sonorous voice, in the formal Polish third-person manner: "Does the lady know me?" he said.

"No, I don't know the gentleman," Lucy replied.

"But I know you!" he burst out. "You are my sister!"

Lucy paused for a moment, as the waitress approached our table. "Can I bring either of you some more coffee?"

My thoughts were racing. So, Peter, chubby little Peter, Lucy's kid brother who could be so vexing at times, had survived and had turned into a handsome young man with a deep melodious voice! "Where is he now and how did he find you?"

"Well, he lives in Wisconsin, and there's quite a story attached to how he found me. I told you that two of my companions decided to leave for Munich. They had hitched a ride on an American vehicle, and the driver, though in American uniform, wore a Polish insignia on his sleeve. After an exchange in Polish, they learned that he was a member of the Free Polish Forces, attached to the American army, and that he, too, was looking for members of his family. From there it was only a question of time until our family name came up and, oh well, you know the rest."

I decided to come to the point of our meeting. A few weeks earlier, out of the clear blue, I had received a phone call from Lucy. She had tracked me down through my writing and wanted me to know, among other things, of her upcoming visit to our hometown. Was there anything she could do for me? After a moment's hesitation, I told her that there was in fact one person to whom I would like to send a small gift. Her name was Irma, and she was the granddaughter of my beloved nanny who had passed away years earlier. I had been in sporadic contact with Irma over the years, but this was a real chance to resume ties with her family.

During our initial phone conversation, Lucy had suggested that I write an introductory letter in Polish; after all, under Poland's Communist regime all foreigners were suspect. Although I had readily agreed to do so, the writing of a letter in Polish had presented a considerable challenge, inasmuch as I had not corresponded in that language in more than thirty years. The few notes I had exchanged with Irma's family had been in German, Bielsko having been a typical European border area, where we had been brought up bilingually. German had dominated our household, though, because our family had lived under Austrian rule for most of their lives. I had procrastinated on the letter until now, and sitting in the maroon-and-gray vinyl booth at the coffee shop, I implored my friend, "Please help me! I am no longer sure of my ground in Polish. How would you put it?"

"Well," she said, "why don't you start out something like this—"

Before she could go on, the Polish words began to tumble onto the page, and to my utter amazement, instead of the usual near-illegible scrawl that had become my trademark, my fingers were tracing that meticulous, precisely rounded script on which I had worked so diligently as a schoolgirl. How I had labored to match the perfect penmanship of the girl with whom I shared a desk throughout elementary school. Even now I found it impossible to articulate her name.

I became aware that Lucy was nervously glancing at her watch, and that interrupted my reverie, bringing me back to reality. We quickly paid the check and made our way back to the terminal and to Lucy's gate, where she became involved in the boarding procedure. Just before parting, she said, "If I should run into Gerta Teppel, what should I tell her?" *There it was! She had spoken the unutterable!*

"Tell her," I sputtered in an infantile outburst of braggadocio hurt, "tell her that I live in the greatest country in the world and that I'm very happily married!" We embraced, and I turned toward the terminal exit.

Once outside, I found a bus that would take me to the Loop area downtown. "Welcome to Chicago. This coach will stop at the Palmer House, the Pick Congress, and Hilton Hotels. The fare is three dollars and fifty cents."

GERTA! GERTA TEPPEL! Knit four, purl two . . . five rows, then switch. Heavy white wool . . . knit four, purl two. Gerta Teppel, my best friend from way back in first grade. We had walked to and from school every day. Gerta and Gerda, the inseparable duo. She had blond hair with bangs which stopped just above her eyebrows. Naturally I had copied her style with my dark bangs. Every morning we would greet each other, "Servus!" then fall into step and cover the fifteen minutes to school in animated conversation. Our desk was designed for two, so we sat next to each other throughout the elementary grades. She was very neat and accomplished in so many things I felt inadequate about. That made me want to emulate her in every way possible. And, it had gotten to the point where, after considerable effort on my part, it was indeed difficult to tell our handwriting apart. She excelled in music and voice, where I drew an almost complete blank. On the other hand, I compensated for that by getting good marks in language and poetry classes—subjects that were difficult for her. Our respective grade averages were nearly always close. Inseparable as we were during school hours, we would rarely meet afterward. Whenever I would broach the subject, she would be noncommittal and make some vague excuse about mysterious-sounding activities that somehow kept her from seeing me. That only heightened my interest in her, and I resolved that there was nothing, but nothing, that I wouldn't do for her.

As we grew older, we naturally began to take an interest in boys, and I developed a crush on a boy named Henek. He had two younger sisters with whom I was friendly. My idol had the bluest eyes, the darkest hair, and a small, upturned nose. He paid no attention to me whatsoever, until one day, during a ping pong game with his sister Lola, it turned out that I beat her. "You play well for a girl your age," he allowed. "Want to play a game with me?" Flustered, I accepted the challenge and promptly missed every ball, dropped my paddle at one point, then stumbled and was forced to crawl under the table to retrieve the ball. I was mortified and, to make matters worse, hit my head coming out from under the table. That provided an excuse to break into tears. Henek, realizing what was happening, gallantly dismissed the incident, "Oh, too bad you hurt your head. We must play another time."

I took my departure through blinding tears and ran home as fast as I could, replaying in my mind all the mistakes I had made and how I could have avoided them. I found Mama in the living room, busily knitting a ski sweater for me, made of heavy white wool. I still see the intricate braid design: knit four, purl two. In the familiar comfort of my surroundings, the fiasco gradually faded.

Later that afternoon Lola arrived at the house to announce that a group of her friends were going skiing the coming Sunday. Could I come along? she wanted to know. Henek would lead us, take us to one of his favorite spots on the mountain. I could hardly believe the turn of events. And Henek would see me in that fabulous sweater! Could I? Would I? "Mama," I begged, "could you finish that sweater by Sunday, please, please?"

"I think I could give it a try," she agreed. After that, the needles fairly flew: knit four, purl two. Wait till I wear that sweater with the navy blue ski pants! And Henek would be there!

Saturdays meant that we had classes only until noon. Gerta and I were walking home from school. A light snow was falling, the prayed-for powdery snow. "You know, I've been thinking," Gerta said. "Wouldn't it be nice to get together this weekend? We could play Tivoli." How many weekends had I tried in vain to get her to come to the house to play that Polish variation of a pinball game! I was overjoyed.

I replied enthusiastically, "Sure. Why don't you come over right now? First we can have lunch and then spend the afternoon doing fun things."

"I'm sorry, I can't make it right now, but I'll come over tomorrow afternoon. My parents will be at a wedding then."

For a fleeting moment, it occurred to me that she might have heard about our ski plans, but I also realized that she could never go skiing because of a leg injury. I couldn't very well ask her to come along anyway—her limp made that too difficult. I had a terrible dilemma. I was dying to go with Henek. He would be impressed with the way I skied, and, with me wearing that new sweater, he had to notice me, just *had* to. On the other hand, how selfish of me to want to be on those slopes while my best friend had to stay home alone. No, my sacrifice for her would certainly cement our friendship, or would it? I vacillated. In the end, Gerta won out.

Sunday came, and the snow had improved overnight. Its crystal grains were glistening in the sun like confectioner's sugar. Mama was delighted that I had decided against going skiing. She viewed any sport with a great deal of apprehension, fear of accidents being the predominant factor. In honor of the occasion, she had prepared a sumptuous lunch for us. Mama possessed that rare quality of treating her children's friends as she would her own special guests. We devoured the marble cake, drank the cocoa, and thus fortified, focused on the intricacies of Tivoli for a while. To my acute disappointment, Gerta left much earlier than I had anticipated. Although it had been a nice afternoon, I felt that I had not been wholly satisfying. Idly I went up to my room and lay on my bed in the darkness of the winter afternoon, staring moodily at the barely discernible shape of my white sweater on the dresser.

A FEW YEARS LATER, DURING THE SWELTERING SUMMER OF 1940, well into the war and the German occupation of Poland, an errand took me—the yellow Jewish star prominently affixed to my blouse, as decreed by the occupying Nazi forces—to the post office. Just then, coming down the brown sandstone steps of the building, I spied Gerta. She was wearing a blue dress with a mushroom print pattern. Looking around furtively, and finding no one in sight, I held my voice to a minimum: "Gerta!" She looked straight at me. "Gerta!" I repeated, a note of urgency and trepidation creeping into my voice. Her eyes looked straight through me and without stopping for a moment, she said, "I don't talk to Jews!"

None of the subsequent beatings at the hands of the Nazi guards, or the insidious indoctrination lectures, designed to acquaint us with our lower-than-low status in the Aryan order of evolution, were to inflict as much pain as this rejection, coming from a friend I had once adored. It was as if I had found a shameful and inimical flaw in myself that would forever condemn me to be a pariah. After that I never uttered her name again, and during all the years that followed, had totally excised her from my mind.

THE AIRPORT BUS STOPPED IN FRONT OF MY HOTEL ON MICHIGAN AVENUE. Getting off, I found myself unable to enter the building. Instead I wandered the busy street. Looming up ahead was a subway entrance and, on an impulse, I went below. It was cold, clammy, and not entirely unlike a dungeon. The moist stones echoed the sound of footsteps. I felt out of sorts and emotionally drained. Walking tentatively up to a ticket window, I stopped short, changed my mind, quickly turned, and fled. People were going about their busy lives and to their various destinations, and I felt cast adrift. Over on the other side, I saw a stairway leading up to the street. Next to the bottom steps, the forlorn figure of a man leaned against the wall. In front of him stood a small tin bucket that held some flowers swathed in green tissue paper. I was instinctively drawn toward him, but as I got closer, I noticed a circle of petals all around him. The flowers were wilted. I passed him without stopping and made my way up the stairs.

Outside the sun was bright, and I walked along the avenue in aimless pursuit of . . . what? Eventually, I found myself sitting on a stool at a deli counter. The waitress approached. "What are you going to have?" she challenged perfunctorily. My eyes fell on a yogurt ad, and I indicated my choice.

"What kind?" she pressed on as I hesitated. "The blueberry is very good," she suggested helpfully.

"Okay, blueberry then."

She briskly walked away, and over the counter, I could see that her legs were heavily bandaged. In a few moments she was back. "Here we are—it's nice and fresh."

"Thanks very much."

I didn't want to stay there too long, and on my prompting, she wrote out the check. It came to seventy-eight cents. I put two dollars on the counter, which produced a quizzical look. She pushed one of the dollar bills toward me.

"It's okay," I said. "Keep it!"

"Anything wrong, hon?" she inquired, her eyes troubled.

"No, nothing. It's just that you're very nice." I got up, went outside, and resumed my aimless stroll. After an interval, I found myself in front of my hotel entrance, over which hung several flags. The late afternoon sunlight warmed my face and arms, and somehow the flags felt comforting.

DURING THAT NIGHT, I AWOKE SEVERAL TIMES, vicariously experiencing Lucy's flight. I lived through her takeoff to the East, the long flight across the dark waters of the Atlantic, saw the bright, silent, starry sky. She is getting ever closer to Bielsko. I lived there once, a long time ago. When I saw it last, its rooftops were glistening wet in the sunlight after I had just been brutally torn from my mother. That was a stage on my way to the slave labor and concentration camps. Would Lucy be with Irma tomorrow, in that same house where Irma's mother and grandmother had spent their lives? Would she be ascending those stairs I had run up so many times as a little girl? That handbag that had rested between us in the coffee shop at O'Hare. Would she put it on my nanny's chair? Through the window she would be able to see our house, our rooms, the garden with the gnarled plum tree from which I used to swing, and where I bade a last good-bye to my childhood on a wet April morning. Was it all still there?

I had told Lucy of a picture that used to hang over my bed when I was growing up. It depicted a dark-haired girl in a diaphanous white dress, stretching her arms toward a rose arbor, but an angel was shielding her eyes. In this day and age such bittersweet depictions would be considered the epitome of romantic kitsch. But memory has a way of playing strange tricks on us, and through the rose-colored window of recollection, I see it as being lovely and poignant. It brings back Mama's soft voice, her attempt to explain to me that it meant one should not wish to look into the future. We had left it with Irma's grandmother when we had to move to the Bielsko ghetto.

"If you should find that picture, please buy it for me at any price," had been my plea to Lucy. But that morning, after a night of searching for answers, I knew I no longer wanted it.

Artur/Columbine

OCTOBER 19, 2000, LITTLETON, COLORADO

*O*VER DECADES OF LIVING A NORMAL LIFE, I learned that the naive hope I had once nurtured and fully believed in was never to be realized. It was a simple hope: that no one—after coming to understand the gratuitous horror, suffering, and loss inflicted on millions of people during World War II—would ever be cruel, indifferent, or foolhardy enough to wage war again. However, given the long record of mankind's prejudices, national and religious fervor, as well as political ambitions, I sadly had to conclude that my hope was futile. That left me to pick up the pieces and attempt to make the best of my life. But a few happenings shook me to my very foundations. They are the incidents we have seen that are rooted in blind hatred and intolerance, premeditated and committed for some imagined personal wrongs; to punish, to kill wantonly and mercilessly. That is the same ruthless murder by which my family and millions of others died, something with which I shall never come to terms.

It devastated me to realize that such evil can also exist in our country in the present. First came the atrocity at Oklahoma City. When I traveled there, I wept at the fenced enclosure, looking at the teddy bears and other stuffed animals and childish poems, left by good and compassionate people. By the time Columbine happened, it echoed in a resounding way. Ultimately, Kurt and I were invited to go there for our first visit on January 20, 2000—exactly nine months to the day after the tragedy. It was a great honor for us to be invited.* Soon, though, a number of grave concerns surfaced. Would my story of coping with tragedy turn out to

---

* By Rita Schaefer of McDougal Littell.

131

be contradictory to the advice and counseling the students and faculty had received from accredited professionals?

When I posed that question to Frank DeAngelis, the principal, and to Gordon and Ellin Hayes, teachers closely involved with the students who had died, they assured me that I could and should just be myself. That turned out to be not too difficult. The kids showed an almost intuitive understanding of my experience and realized that I knew what they had lived through. I, too, was fifteen when I saw my friends killed in cold blood in the name of Hitler, as they had seen on that horrible April 20, in honor of Hitler's birthday, when their "friends" killed so many of them for the same reason. I understand their pain, their loss, their anguish, for I too have asked myself, countless times, how someone I was sitting next to at lunch, with whom I walked to school, could plan my cold-blooded murder over a protracted period of time.

That was a question I couldn't answer, but I could and did answer another: Can you, after what you have seen, after what you have lost, build a life again, laugh again? The answer is a resounding yes. I held those wounded young people in my arms and assured them from my own experience that a full and rich life was still ahead of them. Yes, they would always remember, scars would remain, and the memory of those events would be painful. I cautioned them that anything could and probably would trigger it, but they would also see their lives and their environs in a different light. The colors of flowers would be deeper, the stars shine brighter; every day would be more precious. They must not say, I can't do this because of what I have been through, but rather, Yes, I can do it, because I have seen the worst, and I can help to make things better. Pain should not be wasted; pain can be used to heal. They trusted me, because they knew that I had been there.

I believe that those affected at Columbine realized that I understood what had so ruthlessly been taken from them: not only their friends but the image they had held dear of the place they loved. Columbine, the school where graduations and dances were held; columbine, the flower, tender and beautiful, growing from the rugged strength of the Rocky Mountains, unblemished, fragile. Whenever the name Columbine is uttered now, it conveys the image of carnage, of backpacks from which not only a yellow pencil protrudes but a lethal gun as well. I know that particular pain. I know and hate the image so often seen on the TV screen, of pitifully emaciated people with huge, vacant, hungry eyes. Often when I am being introduced as a Holocaust survivor, with all that that conjures in people's minds, I would like to cry out, No, that is not the person I am! After all, I was not born as a number. That is not the image I want you to retain of me. I had a name, parents, a childhood, a home, and a life filled with beauty and caring.

I understand why the victims of the Columbine tragedy want the beauty of that name restored. More so, they want to be identified as what they are—vital young people with caring, loving hearts—rather than have the label "tragic victims" imposed upon them. They want to give back some of the outpouring of friendship and understanding the world has heaped upon them. In that way, tragedy can be a catalyst for change—change for the better.

Whenever I enter a school and see kids with their backpacks going in and out, alone or in clusters—exuberant, comfortable, and seemingly safe—my heart quickens with an undefined fear of the distant past still echoing in my mind. It gives me a new measure of the preciousness of time. Tied to it is a personal memory of what happened to me as a teenager on October 19, 1939, and then exactly sixty-one years later.

THE AIR IS SLIGHTLY CHILLY. Burnished leaves crunch under my feet, and clouds gather in the blue October sky. My eyelids sting from barely suppressed tears, and my thoughts are far away. I have just emerged from Columbine High School, from the immaculate halls of the newly rebuilt library, whose high ceiling is crowned by a breathtaking mural: soaring toward that apex are aspen trees, their roots firmly grounded; thus secured, they reach for the sky. There, far above, they form a crown, a halo, offering a glimpse of sky touched by a few tentative rays of sun—a symbol of hope.

Inside I held a young man of about seventeen in my arms. A boy still, whose life's trust, security, and joy have been shattered by what he has witnessed: wanton brutality, fanned by blind hatred. He has seen lives arbitrarily snuffed out, and his soul is burdened by self-doubt and by the guilt of survival. I see his pain, his sorrow, the unspoken and unanswered questions in his eyes, and I understand. I hold him in my arms and tell him that, yes, the pain will ultimately fade, though scars will remain. He will be able to take that pain, that understanding, and use it. Turn the pain into healing, I told him. Has my pain healed me? Or allowed me to help others? No matter. Pain was an indispensable part of my recovery. I hold him tight, the boy with unshed tears in his eyes, his trembling lips attempting to smile, and I walk out into the chilly October air, my feet scuffing through the fallen leaves.

My thoughts take me far away, to this exact same day in October, sixty-one years before, when my nimble feet swept over the fallen leaves from the trees in the garden of my childhood, to which I fled after my final embrace with another young man. The memory remains of his bright eyes bravely warding off the tears, his trembling lips attempting to smile while he held me tight. I was looking up at him, searching for comfort from him, my big brother, who had always seemed able to solve my problems. On that October day, he was on the brink of manhood, and I was just fifteen.

I have thought of him ceaselessly, looked for him, prayed for his survival, knowing how slim those hopes were. So many reminders have evoked a moment shared with him, and I have cried and longed for him every day of every year. How many days does that make? Too many to count, and it would be to no avail to add them up. How many memories are with me of the brief time we were granted to be together? How much, much more could we have shared, had fate been kinder? I have always looked for him, and I still do, although with now much-diminished hope. He would be an old man, over eighty, whereas the last time I saw him he was nineteen. I have tried to picture what he would look like, but my inner field of vision allows me to see him only as he was then: tall, slim, his glossy hair as black as a raven's wing, coming to a peak in the middle of his prominent high forehead. His eyes were brown, warm as melted chocolate. Whenever he laughed, the mirth would dance in his eyes an instant before it touched his lips. His teeth were white and even.

I cannot envision him as an old man. Yet, when I look into the mirror and see myself as I am now, I cannot deny what time has wrought. That young, slim, long-legged girl with the dimpled, freckled face belongs to another life. Throughout the decades, I have watched the changes of growing from the teen he knew to a young woman—pretty, I was told—enhanced by the bloom of youth and the radiance of love. There followed contentment and fulfillment when my children were born and I matured. I pictured him, Artur, as he was then, and growing older, a handsome man with silver threads in his black hair. In the course of my frequent travels, I always looked for him. It was easier, somehow, to give expression to my fantasies when I was away from home. Unfettered by daily obligations, I could dream of finding him and what our reunion would be like. I would invent a thousand scenarios and wonder what we would say to each other at our encounter after such an interval. In every hotel room, in countless cities, I would peruse the phone book, sometimes finding an Artur Weissmann, but never daring to cross the tenuous line between hope and reality by picking up the receiver. I could never force myself to make that call. How much easier to daydream during flights, when the earth below was invisible and the expanse of sky did not hem in my dreams.

THE LAST TIME I HAD HEARD FROM HIM WAS IN 1943. After the end of the war in 1945, his part of Eastern Europe was cut off by the Iron Curtain, and it was easy to imagine him to be in the Soviet Union, unable to communicate with the West. That was the main reason I never attempted to Americanize my name, as would have been possible at the time of my naturalization. I had turned the idea over in my mind, but instead I always used my maiden name as my middle name, so that he would more easily be able to find me. When Soviet science burst into prominence, I hung my slim, immature hope on the fact that he, who had always been interested in science, had perhaps pursued it, might even have become famous for his work. And so I contrived a scenario that would allow him the possibility of attending a scientific seminar in a city to which I would be traveling as well, and that I would come upon him unexpectedly. I dwelled on every minute detail of such a meeting, often inventing drawbacks that might surface, a sense of estrangement that might set in. What would happen if he had become a hardheaded, indoctrinated Russian scientist and I a patriotic American? Would our loyalties to our adopted countries tear us apart? I used to spend a lot of time on that, but always resolved it by evoking memories of our parental home, our shared years of childhood and adolescence. He would break into laughter when I would remind him how he used to say that someday he would be the first man on the moon, just so he could get away from my constant chatter. I had never quite fallen for that, as I would point out to him, but I always knew that he would achieve some greatness, as indeed he had in my fantasies.

When the first Sputnik orbited the earth, the newspaper published the time when it would pass over our city. I would steal in to my children's rooms, open their windows, and let whatever dim reflection of that manmade star brush over their sleep-enveloped faces, convinced that if he had been instrumental in its creation, it would be good. Surely he would never hurt my children.

But more often a memory would stir, triggered by the echo of some distant laughter. Once an entire scene came vividly to life when I spotted a billboard advertising a certain brand of shaving cream. It brought to mind how he had been shaving with his as yet unpracticed hand, and I had come up to taunt him about it, mimicking an absurd ad I had seen in our Polish magazines. It depicted a prickly, stubble-faced cactus that bellowed a jingle. How I had screeched, "Sharpies shave, no nick this time/Sharpies shave in the nick of time!" I repeated the inane words of my singsong over and over to annoy him. Finally, unnerved, he cut his chin, and his patience snapped. A trace of blood was streaking over the white shaving soap. He put down the razor, and I ran out to the garden, Artur in hot pursuit until he caught me. With his left hand he pinned both of my arms behind my back; then, slowly and deliberately, he lathered my face. At the same time, he gave his rendition of the crazy jingle, with an authentic intonation. He was not satisfied until he had lathered my entire face and neck, while I tried desperately and in vain to wriggle out of his grip. But even in his anger, he was careful of my eyes. Finally, he lathered my ears. It was then that I resorted to the weapon that always seemed to disarm him: I began to cry.

So it has been going for decades, for more than half a century. Full-blown incidents of shared memory, of scenes imagined and real, of fragments, shreds, snippets of recollections assail me in the most unlikely situations. He is there, I reach out to him, but my arms are empty and bitter. A loneliness overtakes me, assuaged only in my husband's and children's embrace. I have peered with searching intensity at my children and grandchildren, in the prayerful hope that some of his genes might have found their way into them and have been rewarded. My son inherited much that I loved and admired in my brother, and my grandson, as he matures, bears him a striking resemblance. Am I merely imagining it because I want it so very much? It hurts me to think that there is no one left in the world who knew him, that only I can remember him.

The last few years have diminished my search. I can no longer picture our reunions; only the memory of him sustains me. The pain of loss becomes more acute when I hold before me the image of that young, courageous boy, filled with ideals and dreams. He seemed to possess all the attributes one could hope for: talent, the right instincts and values, and, above all, compassion for others. Again and again I go back to the moment of our parting, during the bitterness of the war. It was as if a sharp knife had cut off my past from the future. He was gone, his shining brightness gone, and with him all the carefree days of my childhood. Without him my dreams were shattered. After that, I lost everything—my parents, my home, the life that had been mine. The war raged on, and only the memory of him was left, as a symbol of all I had loved and lost. From then on I centered my hopes on finding him, believing that he would restore my losses. In that unrealistic world of my daydreams, I felt that he would be truly capable of it. Nothing along those lines would have astonished me. Yet I did draw the boundaries sharply, and found no contradiction in lighting memorial candles for him while still dreaming of finding him. It hurt no one and saw me through difficult times.

Holding the young boy at Columbine in my arms, I thought about my brother, both of them younger than some of my grandchildren, and I realized with awe that I was passing on my brother's message. He had charged me in that last hour to take care of our parents. That became my challenge in the face of nearly insuperable odds. Many times, when I felt at the end of my strength, I remembered his admonition to go on, for his and our parents' sake, and thus I pulled through. It became my mission, my comfort, to mobilize my pain in order to tell others that life still held much promise. That is my brother's legacy, and it is a bond that, in some strange, undefined, mystical way, has retained an intimate connection with him. Perhaps by helping to ease others' pain, I am repaying some stranger's kindness to my brother.

Holding the wounded children of Columbine in my arms, I can tell them to go on, that the memory will be with them, but that they will be strong and can use their painful experience to help others, in the process healing themselves. I am comforted by the thought that they will find closure when standing at the graves of those they loved. In their hearts, they can say, *I am here with you, I remember you.*

I do not know where my brother's grave is. I have whispered the question a thousand times, no matter what the season. My quest goes to the budding trees, to a rushing brook, to the stars at night: Artur, where are you?

_____

More recently, of course, came the tragic events of September 11, 2001, which I discuss in another chapter.

Kurt

*M*Y LOVE. The pillow next to mine, untouched, pristine, ghostly white in the moonlight. Empty. My heart struggles for some hold, some anchor in the vast emptiness that engulfs me. How can emptiness be so heavy and shrill agonizing cries so silent?

Memories, images, flickering like a fast-rolling film, wash over me. I want to hold on to them, but they elude me as swiftly as they come. They retreat into the shadows and leave me bereft and wanting.

My brother's last embrace, his smiling lips, his eyes brimming with unshed tears.

Papa, touching my bangs gently, lovingly, with his large warm fingers, while I lie in my white crib.

Our children laughing on a sun-drenched beach while the waves wash away their half-built sandcastle.

My head heavy on Mama's tear-soaked pillow on our last night together, and my own still-gnawing guilt after more than sixty years for not consoling her, but burying myself in my own selfish need to be comforted after Papa was taken away.

Then you, a thousand times you. The blue of your eyes—my sky. You, when I first saw you, so long, long ago, you, my love—my god. The look on your face, forever etched in my heart, a look of outrage and compassion. And at that first moment, my overwhelming desire to shield you from pain then and ever after. Oh my love, my love! I prayed for you that night, though I did not know your name. I have prayed for you every night of my life since, except the last, in the hospital in Guatemala, when, exhausted, I fell asleep before praying my most sacred, intense prayer, that you might never be taken from me again. God, in your infinite power, you could not be that cruel to take my love from me the next day. Why? Why? I have cried out a thousand times.

Asleep and yet awake, I see you, my love. In a stranger's home at a rain-washed window, standing next to me. I, so ill, so frail, so lonely, so alone. You felt my loneliness; you knew my thoughts; you knew my needs. Gently you wrapped your arm around me. That first, warm, affectionate gesture after three bitter years brought me to tears. You kissed away my tears. You held me gently in your young, strong arms, shielding me from loneliness and pain. Throughout our life together, whenever pain assailed me, you held me. I was never alone again. Memory—blessed, cursed memory. You will never hold me again. How can I go on?

Oh so long ago, when you held me first, I did not know that my liberator, my omnipotent handsome prince from a faraway distant paradise, was a lonely boy. For me you were always strong. When I woke up from horrible nightmares of my past, your arms were there, reassuring me of the reality of my blessed present. And now? When I awake from my dreams, the nightmare of the present engulfs me with its haunting emptiness. The children and all the grandchildren are here. Day and night since you are gone they have been with me and have cared for me, anticipating all my needs, brushing aside everything that could hurt me. I have not been left alone even a single day. Our children and their spouses, who have always been our children, have wept with me, have honored you, have been everything and more we ever dreamed of. Every child and grandchild speaks of you. It should be a solace, but it is a source of pain, because I cannot turn to you and say: "Look." I cannot see the pride in your eyes, that small happy smile around your lips.

I have never lived without hope for a happy ending, even when hope was only an illusion. As long as we were together, we had a happy ending. We reached our summit over morning coffee. No one else understood or knew. And sometimes even you did not know. Was it yesterday or a century ago? At the airport I saw you coming toward me, your raincoat belt dragging on the ground as always, your tie askew, your eyes smiling over your smudged glasses. I ran to you, pulling your belt up, adjusting your tie. "Do you always have to?" you were saying. But did you know that my heart was beating with the same soaring joy it did more than half a century ago?

They say that time will blunt and lessen the pain. No, my love, I want no lessening of the pain, which is intertwined with my love for you. You have never failed me. There was never "you and I." It was always "we." We had our disagreements. We shouted at each other. But never, not once in all our years together, not in our angriest outbursts, though we knew each other's most vulnerable feelings, did we ever touch them. Our love for each other was unconditional because it rested on the bedrock of absolute trust. Rare was the night that we did not sleep in each other's arms.

I reach for you to the empty pillow. Under it is the shirt you wore on the last day. You are not here. I went to your grave. I put my head on the place where I think your head rests. I found a few last drops of Arpège, the first perfume you gave me so long ago and ever since. I put it on my neck, where you loved to smell it on me. I pressed my head onto the grass. It tickled my face as your face did before you shaved. I clutched the ground to be near you as we had been back there in Paris in spring, in the springtime of our lives. You, my young husband. The smell of lilies-of-the-valley. The magic and enchantment of our love. You, my heaven and my earth.

Now you are waiting for me, as I waited for you to return after we parted.

I am in my empty bed again. High over the trees the moon is looking at me from the star-studded sky. The moon, my faithful old friend. The only friend that was free in my years of my slavery. I had confided in it, asked questions. At times it hid its face behind a veil of drifting clouds to avoid, I guess, the answer. But on that day, that blessed day, the happiest of my life, when I confessed that I knew you loved me too, and that we would merge our lives and never be alone again, it beamed its broadest smile. I came to learn that the moon's brightness is but a dim reflection of the sun. That its smile and its frown are bleak, cold, desolate, and lonely. But to me it is still dear; it looks down at both of us. I think of you, my love, and of the time when we will be together again and for all eternity. Our children will come to visit us.

Our grandchildren and their children, too. My only comfort in my grief is that you live on in them. Even in my darkest, most desperate hours, I know that your love was worth my pain.

Letter to
My Grandchildren

I AM FLYING EAST, TOWARD THE MAINLAND, TOWARD HOME.
Below me the Pacific is wrapped in a cloak of darkness, a presence I can only sense without visible proof of its existence. Above me stretches a canopy of star-studded infinity. Thus suspended and alone with my thoughts, I turn to you—the positive, the tangible, the real, the miracle of immortality. I see you, my grandchildren, in my mind's eye, asleep in your beds with night-lights on to ward off the fear of the dark and the unknown with which we all are imbued.

That you can sleep safely and securely is due to the sacrifice of those at whose tomb I stood yesterday.

Yesterday I stood at Pearl Harbor.

Now I am returning from Hawaii, with boxes of macadamia nuts, orchids, and memories.

Diamond Head, chiseled in venerable majesty, stood vigil over the blue-green waters of the Pacific. Behind it Koko Head and the Punchbowl, the fires in their craters long extinguished.

I leave behind the gleaming steel-and-glass towers, the polyglot traffic, the teeming metropolis that is Honolulu.

Aloha, Hawaii. Aloha!

I REMEMBER THE SIGNS: HANAUMA BAY, PUNCHBOWL CRATER, PEARL HARBOR.

Pearl Harbor.

The day is hot. I follow the crowd through the gates and take a number for my tour to be called. I see an elderly man looking around almost dazed, as if searching for someone. I walk in reverence, annoyed that soft drinks are being sold nearby. I wish for quiet and bird song.

This place is sacred—a cemetery, a place of worship. Pearl Harbor, where so many died that more could live. Pearl Harbor, once the gates of hell's fury unleashed, but now again a safe harbor—an anchor for tomorrow.

A hush falls as we enter the auditorium, to see and to understand the events of that day, which made this place a shrine of memory. The theater darkens; the footage runs; the waves wash again and again over coral-encrusted fragments of the ship, the USS *Arizona*, a giant coffin for the boys who sleep their eternal sleep. The waves whisper of yesterday.

SATURDAY NIGHT, DECEMBER 6, 1941.

How handsome the boys look in their immaculate uniforms—their faces so young, so eager for life. A band competition is held ashore. They play and play well, as do the bands of many another vessels of the fleet. Music and laughter mingle in the balmy, starry night. But in the distance, the enemy keeps a silent rendezvous, the aircraft carriers lie in wait with their deadly cargo. Quietly, stealthily, they wait for the dawn, while the bands play onshore. The *Arizona's* band wins second prize and earns the privilege of sleeping late on Sunday, December 7, 1941.

Dawn, sunrise, and another rising sun, on wings of destruction, wreaks havoc among the unsuspecting. The boys who slept late now sleep forever. In the light of a new day, this "Day of Infamy," darkness descends, and 2,409 souls are consumed by fire and water. The Japanese attack planes turn the harbor into a blazing inferno. The *Arizona* sinks within nine minutes, followed by a large part of the unwary fleet. The United States and the empire of Japan are at war.

The Horsemen of the Apocalypse have been reigning supreme in another part of the world for more than two years. Hitler's Germany has enslaved nation after nation. Its ally, Japan, now joins the dance of death that will awaken the "sleeping giant."

The fires of Pearl Harbor like the self-destructive fires of the stars pierce the darkness and become the beacons by which the truth will be illuminated.

I TAKE THE BOAT OUT TO THE MEMORIAL and stand at the *Arizona's* resting place, straining to peer into the waves that are gently washing over the rusty hull, but the sea does not divulge its secrets. I see the fire-twisted smokestack, rising to the water's edge, fastened to it is a bright new mast flying the Stars and Stripes. I look into the water again and again trying to see—what?

On the twisted hull below, something glistens in the sun, which has just come out from behind the clouds. I look again and want to hide my face in shame—there are coins: pennies, nickels, quarters. What unfeeling creatures have thrown this beggar's pittance to the heroes in their watery grave? But suddenly I know, know the feeling of wanting to touch, to communicate, to leave something behind, something I have carried with me.

I have come prepared.

THE DAY AT HOME HAD BEEN COLD AND CLOUDY, with snow flurries dancing from an overcast sky. The trees were devoid of all leaves. Only the evergreens stood fresh in the feeble light on the morning of my departure. Against the house, protected from the wind and snow, sits a rosebush that, year after year, yields the last rose of summer. This time there was no rose, but among the withered stalks I found a petrified, unopened bud, the beauty of its petals never revealed, never touched by the summer sun. Its fragrance never perfumed the air around it. It had been caught unaware, snuffed out by an early frost, its warm beauty arrested forever.

An oil slick still seeps from the bottom of the sea, decades after the proud ship was dealt a death blow. The oil tints the water the hues of the rainbow. It is the rainbow that spanned the Ark after the forty days of the Flood. A promise? An admonition?

I caress the petrified rose with its living heart and toss it gently into the sea.

The sky suddenly darkens; clouds like shrouds or a mourning veil hang over the hills.

The boat comes to take me back to shore. I stand looking toward the Memorial. The flag is flying not at half mast but in full pride of service over the USS *Arizona*, still in commission.

Arizona? It brings to mind the Phoenix, the bird of hope rising from the ashes of destruction. "Remember Pearl Harbor!" was once a battle cry, in those days of darkness. To us, to you, "Remember Pearl Harbor!" remains a greater challenge for tomorrow. May the world in which you grow up never see the likes of another!

In time to come, visit this paradise island; go, pay your own tribute, stand with respect, with awe, and with a prayer of thanks at the graves of those who died there that you might live in freedom, as your grandmother did this winter's day.

I think of the boys I left behind, who would by now have been old men. What would their lives have held? Achievements? Disappointments? Sorrows and joys? I have only one wish for them: that, as I was doing now, they had had a chance to go home.

Song of the Earth

A Poem by Kurt Klein

The moment captured by capricious choice,
Frozen in time, stunning the eye
through which it coursed so many years ago
by its inadvertent revelations.

Photo by Kurt Klein, photographic enhancements by Alvin Gilens

Under the glass, the scene becomes magnified
In this remote, abandoned childhood kingdom;
The kitchen attains dimension, a mock-proximity,
At once palpable and keeping its rigid distance.

I must ask now, as if the question posed
would suffice to unravel the inexplicable events
and we should have a replay; another beginning
and, certainly, another end: *"Why?"*

The years have made you younger, Father.
To think that I have surpassed your days,
have known fulfillment of what for you
was always to remain a distant dream:

To feel the touch of yet another generation.
You look into the lens, your thoughts
inscrutable at this late stage;
bald-pated and about to sip your

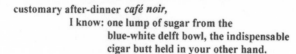

     customary after-dinner *café noir,*
         I know: one lump of sugar from the
             blue-white delft bowl, the indispensable
             cigar butt held in your other hand.

I never noticed as a boy, watching you groom it,
how much your moustache resembled that of your

ex-emperor's, for whom you fought during the
first of two great global conflagrations.

In due time, your country rewarded you for valor
by tearing you from roots, from basic pursuits,
on half an hour's summons by the *Gauleiter*,
hauling you to one of hell's antechambers

somewhere in the Pyrenees - - and then...?
But first. There would be a moment now recalled:
You, standing on the far bank of the river Styx,
full of dark foreboding about this final parting.

And I, floating toward the distant shore
called Life, tossed toward the promontory
of the Promised Land, access to which - -
try as you might - - would ever be denied you.

150

And you, Mother,
        your gentle face set somber
and out of character, as well it might be;
your ready smile, your resolute strength
forced into hiding by the dictates of harsh times.

I see you, a bewildered real-life Alice,

        lost behind the icy prism of the unyielding
        looking glass, your world about to be undone
        by powers far beyond the ken of ordinary people.

Gerda   Weissmann   Klein

That home-baked cake in your careworn hand:
plums of a bitter, much-diminished harvest,
plucked from the tree outside the window
during that haunted fall of thirty-six.

I want to shout in perfect hindsight - - a child,
mesmerized by the ultimate Punch and Judy show:
Watch out - - behind you! Can you not read
the symbols of the writing on the wall?

Look at that Calendar of Jewish Cultural Events
behind your back, agenda of delusive normalcy!
Could you not heed Mahler's impassioned outcry
before his *Lied* turned into one of lamentation?

"Dark is life...is death."

Theme in a minor key, *obbligato* to the demons
of the thirties, the furies of the forties.
Would that you had related it
to your own small plot of earth.

But in the end, would all this culture,
every quirk of history have cautioned you
against the cataclysm of a decade of
blind hatred and destruction, run amuck?

Throughout the years of anguish I was
to learn of your nobility of spirit which
fairly lept from the pages of your tortured,
selfless letters which kept coming for a while
with their hidden code of desperation.
And when my own tormented scribbling
was returned, stamped "Address Unknown'
my mind cried out: O, but I know it well,

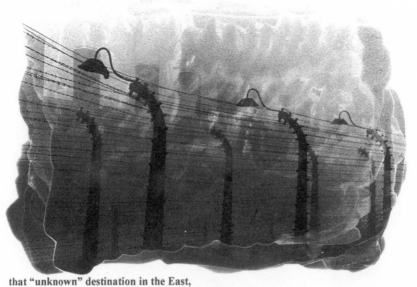

that "unknown" destination in the East,
the trembling that is Treblinka,
the obscenity that is Auschwitz!
What has remained elusive is, *Why?*